BUSINESS INFORMATION PROCESSING

David Harrison

Pitman

PITMAN PUBLISHING LIMITED
128 Long Acre, London WC2E 9AN

A Longman Group Company

© David Harrison 1986

First published in Great Britain 1986

British Library Cataloguing in Publication Data
Harrison, David, 1951–
  Business information processing.
  1. Business data processing
  I. Title
  658′.05   HF5548.2

ISBN 0–273–02440–X

Printed in Great Britain at The Bath Press, Avon

Contents

Preface

It has been said that time becomes more important as the ability to measure it becomes more accurate. Once it was sufficient for the farmer to lean on a gatepost, chew on a straw, examine the sky and say it must be about autumn time. Now it is necessary to keep track of time, at least to the nearest minute, to make sure that appointments are kept. People wear watches capable of measuring time to 1/100th of a second. Time is money and being able to measure time could be the difference between profit and loss.

A similar situation exists with information processing. People managed their business affairs in the days when the few people who could read and write were usually shut away in monasteries. Developments in mechanisms for collecting and processing information over the years have made it necessary to become efficient data processors to survive in commerce and industry.

This text gives a guided tour of a number of different situations in which data processing is carried out and indicates the manner in which information is produced and used.

It is not intended as a definitive work, many gaps have been left and research has to be carried out by the reader but this gives an opportunity to acquire some of the skills which will be necessary for successful employment in the future, the ability to be flexible and adapt to new situations, accept new developments without the restrictions imposed by the discipline of using old skills in a traditional way.

Acknowledgements

I would like to express my gratitude to the following organisations for help and material which they have provided to enable this book to be produced.

Apricot Computers PLC
Associated Examining Board
Banking Information Services
Barclays Bank PLC
Cambridge University Local Examinations Syndicate
Directel Ltd
East Anglian Examinations Board
Holiday Inn
Honeywell
IBM UK LTD
Joint Matriculation Board
London Regional Examining Board
Midland Bank PLC
National Cash Registers
National Westminster Bank
University of Oxford Delegacy of Local Examinations
Southern Regional Examinations Board
West Midlands Examinations Board

Introduction

You are Joe Smith, having recently left full-time education with business studies qualifications and the world to explore. Fortunately you have obtained a job as trainee manager with a motor dealer but your boss, John Jackson, insists that a vital part of your training should include being involved in a number of jobs at ground level. This is why you find yourself looking after the spare parts department where you are responsible for stock control. The job may not be terribly exciting at present but it does pay well and gives you the opportunity to go away on holiday and live reasonably. At present the company is getting into new technology in a big way and that is interesting as well as giving you useful experience. You can also look forward to being your own boss when you take over as manager. In the meantime you make the best of whatever opportunities come your way and take great interest in new developments, including several outside the motor industry.

1 A small business system – Westpool Motor Company

Westpool Motor Company is the company you work for. It is a main agent for cars produced by the Japanese Hotsun company and as such it sells cars and spare parts as well as acting as a regional distribution centre. Garages in the area get their Hotsun cars and spares through Westpool Motors.

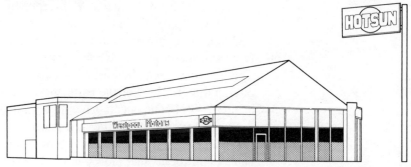

The main function of the company is to sell cars, which it does through the showroom, but in order to provide a good service to customers it must support this function by running a workshop which will carry out general repair and maintenance work on any cars.

Spare parts required by the workshop are taken from the stores but they also supply spare parts to other garages in the area and to the do-it-yourself motorist who has bought a Hotsun car and services and maintains it himself.

Paperwork and administration are looked after by the office, or to be more precise by Brenda Helpfull who is the secretary and who occupies a room connected to the main showroom.

1.1 Stock control

At present you are responsible for managing the stores. This is basically a warehouse which keeps a stock of parts and equipment. To become a main agent for Hotsun, the company insists that you carry a large number of parts. Hotsun are very aware of their image in the market place and when they started to sell cars in Britain ten years ago they were severely criticised because spare parts were not available. The situation is made worse by the fact that they continually change the specifications of the cars that they produce. This has led to the present situation where a very large number of different parts have to be stocked to cover the requirements of the range of cars produced. In fact Westpool stock about 10 000 different items, ranging from nuts and bolts to major engine and transmission assemblies.

One of the first things that you have become aware of since taking over the stores is that stock control is a very delicate operation. You must make sure that sufficient items are held to enable your customers to get what they want immediately. If you cannot supply a customer from outside with the part that he wants, he will buy it somewhere else. When he finds that the part is unobtainable in the area, the reputation of Hotsun suffers, and the customer buys a different make of car next time. Similarly if the workshop cannot be supplied with a part that it requires, repairs cannot be carried out and a customer's car may be off the road for a while. Again this is not good for the reputation of either Hotsun or Westpool Motors.

One answer to this problem is to carry massive stocks of everything to ensure that you can always supply customers with what they want. This requires a lot of storage space for which the company has to pay rates and rent. Many of the parts are delicate, though this is not always obvious. Steel components have to be stored very carefully away from damp or they will rust. Other components may be similarly affected and customers will not take kindly to being supplied with rusty new components. This means that money has to be spent to ensure that the storage areas are warm and dry. Obviously the smaller the area required for storage the cheaper this is. The problem of stock control is that you must juggle permanently with the levels to ensure that you have the minimum number of each item required to give all your customers a good service. Then just as you think you have got the problem solved a crisis comes along. You have been waiting for a delivery of oil filters which should arrive today by rail. Unfortunately the railwaymen have decided to hold a one-day strike, so there will be no deliveries. Fortunately your stock control system has catered for this, and you did not wait until you were out of stock before you placed the order. You have enough filters in stock to last until the next delivery arrives. This is called **safety stock** (Fig. 1.1).

When you arrived to take over the stores you found that your predecessor had a system organised which allowed you to keep a close check on the items that you have in stock. Each item is allocated a bin number and associated with this is a card in a card index system. This card is laid out as shown in Fig. 1.2.

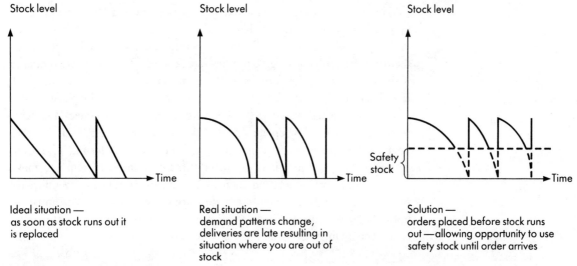

Stock level | Stock level | Stock level

Ideal situation —
as soon as stock runs out it
is replaced

Real situation —
demand patterns change,
deliveries are late resulting in
situation where you are out of
stock

Solution —
orders placed before stock runs
out —allowing opportunity to use
safety stock until order arrives

Fig. 1.1 Stock replacement patterns

STOCK CARD

Item Code _ _ _ _ _ _ _ _ _ _   Description _ _ _ _ _ _ _ _ _ _ _ _ _ _

Supplier _ _ _ _ _ _ _ _ _ _ _ _ _ _ _   Bin No. _ _ _ _ _ _ _

Min. level _ _ _ _ _ _ _ _ _ _   Re-Order Qty. _ _ _ _ _ _ _ _ _ _ _ _ _

Unit size _ _ _ _ _ _ _ _ _ _

Date	Quantities			Date	Quantities		
	IN	OUT	ON HAND		IN	OUT	ON HAND

Fig. 1.2 Stock card

Whenever an item is removed from stock the card index system is updated by writing in the date, and the quantity removed from stock in the quantity out column. Then the quantity removed is subtracted from the quantity on hand to give the new stock level. This value is compared with the minimum level to see if the item needs reordering. If the stock level falls below the minimum, an order for that item must be placed.

You have issued instructions to the storeman always to check for items requiring ordering when he updates the stock cards. As he is human, he may forget or he may mislay his list of items for reordering. The result is that one of your jobs is to go through the card index system and make out a reorder list which can then be passed to Brenda in the office for processing. Whenever goods are delivered the stock records must be updated by writing in the date and the quantity of goods put into stock. Again the quantity on hand must be updated.

Assignment 1

1 Obtain copies of the Westpool stock card and fill in the details of the stock items given in Table 1 below. Order these cards so that they are in ascending item code sequence.

2 Table 2 gives details of a typical sample of transactions taken over a period. Use these details to update your stock cards. Be careful to ensure that goods received are indicated in the IN column and these values are added to the goods on hand. Items issued are noted in the OUT column and these values are subtracted.

Table 1

Item code	Description	Supplier	Bin No.	Min Level	Reorder Qty.	Unit Size	Qty in Stock
A3343340	Head gasket	Hotsun	7	5	20	1	9
A7528140	Oil filter	Hotsun	125	10	50	1	11
B8313733	C.V. joint	Hotsun	453	5	20	1	6
A7528124	Oil pump	Hotsun	127	3	10	1	7
C3397998	Brake pads	Hotsun	203	10	30	2	8
Z1679872	10 mm × 1.5 cm bolts	CK Eng.	95	6	25	12	8
C8327483	Brake hose	Hotsun	173	10	30	1	25
E4382188	Door handle	Hotsun	208	5	10	1	8
X0393738	Sun roof	Carkit	143	2	5	1	1
A4342844	Rocker gasket	Hotsun	169	5	25	1	20
B3318362	Gear lever	Hotsun	183	2	5	1	6
Z6603610	Bleed nipples	CK Eng.	562	5	5	4	5
A3335771	Valve springs	Hotsun	481	5	5	8	5
A684586X	Ign. unit	Hotsun	392	4	5	1	5

Sample of details from stock cards

Table 2

		Quantity	
Date	Item Code	In	Out
12/10/84	A7528124		1
12/10/84	C3397998	30	
12/10/84	E4382188		4
12/10/84	B8313733		1
12/10/84	C8327483		2
13/10/84	X0393738		1
13/10/84	B8313733		1
13/10/84	X0393738	5	
13/10/84	A7528124		2
15/11/84	C8327483		2
18/11/84	C3397998		1
20/11/84	B8313733	20	
20/11/84	A4342844		1
20/11/84	C8327483		2
20/11/84	Z6603610		4
23/11/84	A7528124		1
03/01/85	C3397998		1
05/01/85	A4342844		1
05/01/85	X0393738		1
05/01/85	A3343340		1
08/03/85	B8313733		4
12/04/85	B3318362		1

Random sample of stores transactions

3 Produce a reorder list to be passed on to the office. If the quantity on hand is greater than the minimum reorder level, there is sufficient stock. Where the quantity on hand is below the minimum required, the item must be reordered. The reorder list should contain the item codes, descriptions, name of supplier as well as the quantity to order and unit size.

4 Discuss the following points with other members of your group. You may find it useful to make some notes as a result of this discussion.

a) What would happen if the same stock item was produced in a number of different unit sizes?

b) Every year the stores have to go through a stocktaking procedure. This involves counting the items on the shelves and checking the numbers against those on the stock record. On some occasions, there are fewer items than those recorded. Accountants tend to call this 'slippage'. Discuss the ways in which this discrepancy may occur.

1.2 Microfilm

The stock control system works well within the stores but when you first started working there you wondered how the storeman found anything. The system is easy in theory. Given the part number or item code you can look up the stock records and find out if the required item is in stock (Fig. 1.3). You can then find the bin number and go to the container

Fig. 1.3 Microfilm of stock at Westpool Motors

and bring out the number of items requested. The problem is knowing the part number to begin with.

Years ago all the major motor manufacturers produced catalogues of all the parts which made up each section of their cars. This was fine when the specification changed little from year to year and most car makers only produced a small range of vehicles. However, Hotsun changes models on a regular basis and the design of parts may vary within the same model range. So producing printed catalogues would be expensive, and reprinting them to take the changes into account would be almost impossible. The cost of distributing the catalogues to dealers and agents would also be prohibitive. Still a catalogue of some sort is required if you are to find these part numbers. The answer to the problem is to produce catalogues on microfilm, and Hotsun has a computer which prints lists very quickly. Film is made from computer output and every month an update to the parts list arrives through the post in the form of a number of sheets of film. Each sheet is only 15 cm by 10 cm yet it contains 240 A4 pages of information. This means that the catalogues and updates can be sent cheaply by post. The pages are so small that you cannot read them unaided. Still, on the counter in the stores you have a microfiche reader which looks like a television set and magnifies each page, so that you can read the information.

When a customer arrives at the counter he explains what he wants. You find the relevant microfilm sheet and pull out a small drawer at the base of the reader. The sheet of film is placed on the carrier inside and the drawer is closed. When the machine is switched on the screen lights up and the pages are displayed on the screen. By moving a handle attached to the film carrier it is possible to select the required page. It is then an easy task to find the required part number. With a little bit of practice this can be as fast as looking up the information in a book.

Assignment 2

1   Visit a library which uses microfilm and use a reader to look up pages of information. You may have to ask the librarian for permission to do this.

2   Choose a filing system that you have come across in your school or college. One example may be the storage of old examination papers or scripts. Write a report for the head of the relevant department detailing the advantages and disadvantages of using microfilm for this purpose. You will need to have an idea of the equipment that will be required, and a rough estimate of costs would be useful. Information can be obtained from local office machine suppliers or by writing to the manufacturers of microfilm equipment. Other useful sources of information are the various office equipment magazines and catalogues. The assignment should be presented as a formal report.

Glossary

bin   A store location in a warehouse which contains goods. It may be simply the name of a position in store or it may refer to a container for parts.

microfiche   Sheet of microfilm containing a number of printed pages.

quantity on hand   Actual number of a particular item in stock.

reorder list A list of goods which are in short supply. This usually means that they have reached their safety stock level and need to be ordered from supplier or manufacturer.

safety stock The number of items held when an order for replacements is made. The safety stock may be put on sale while the order is being processed, ensuring that you do not run out of stock completely.

stock card Card index record giving details of each item in store and the number of issues and receipts.

stock control The process of carefully maintaining the quantity of items held within a system to ensure that sufficient stock is available to customers.

2 Westpool Motor Company's computer system

A little while after you had started working for Westpool your boss, John Jackson, came to see you to discuss the possibility of buying a computer to handle the stock control. He had already gained some experience of computers because he had bought a word processor for the office and Brenda found it very useful for a number of tasks. Following the successful introduction of that machine he was looking for similar success in other areas of the business. He knew that you had done some computing while you were at college and wanted you to be involved in installing the new system.

The first thing that you discussed was the type of application for which it would be needed. You explained that computers were general purpose machines capable of a number of different tasks. It was very important therefore that the machine should be adaptable to carry out all the applications which were envisaged. The capability of the machine depended on two things. These were the hardware configuration which is a technical way of saying the type of machine and the software or programs available for that machine. It was decided that it must be capable of handling the stock control for the stores to start with and that it must also be capable of doing the wages and perhaps some accounting at a later date.

2.1 Hardware

Most of the computers on the market tend to follow a common layout which is practically the same as the scheme devised by John von Neumann in the 1940s when the development of computers began. The general layout can be as shown in Fig. 2.1.

Computers vary in size and power. Since the mid 1970s it has been possible to get machines in which the functions of the arithmetic unit and the control unit are carried out by a single device. This is known as a microprocessor chip and consists of a thin wafer of silicon containing the equivalent of the thousands of electronic components required to perform the tasks in older machines. This is just one example of the type of component known as an integrated circuit. The use of other integrated circuits in units making up a computer system has meant that computers can be very small and at the same time very powerful.

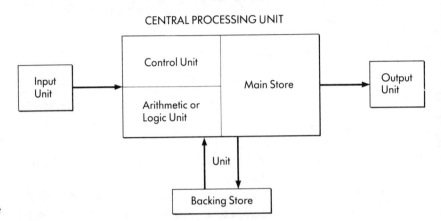

Fig. 2.1 A computer layout

You spent a lot of time visiting computer dealers with John once you had decided what you wanted of the machine. Many of the computers that you saw were not suitable. These tended to be described as 'home micros' and consisted of a very good processing unit with a limited amount of memory, a keyboard for input and a television screen to display the output. Backing store was usually in the form of a domestic tape cassette unit. John was quite interested in these machines because they were very cheap.

However, you explained that many of them would not suit him because they had limited memory size. Memory is measured in kilobytes (or K for short), and each character that you type on the keyboard, or read from a tape cassette requires one byte of storage. A kilobyte consists of 1024 bytes or characters and the more kilobytes a machine can store in its main memory the more useful it is likely to be. Some of the home computers had memories limited to 16K or 32K. John would probably require at least 64K of memory to enable him to run the programs he required.

A further disadvantage in the machines at the cheap end of the market was the backing store. Information stored in the main memory of the computer is lost when the power is turned off. This is called volatile memory, and is a technical limitation of the components used to make up the memory. So any information that you are likely to require over again such as programs, or the stores stock file, would have to be stored in a backing store which is more permanent. The usual way of doing this is to save the information on a magnetic medium. It is exactly the same as making a tape recording of a piece of music. The notes are recorded and remain permanently stored so that they can be played back at any time. The domestic tape recorder provides a cheap simple method of storing information for this purpose. The problem is that the recording starts at the beginning of the tape and subsequent information is recorded sequentially as on the tracks on a music cassette. When it is time to recover the information you have to start at the beginning and move through the cassette until you come to the required data. This can take a very long time and is not very convenient. It may be suitable for storing games programs, but it is not terribly useful for businesses where speed is a major reason for using the computer in the first place.

It did not prove too difficult to find machines capable of handling the work that John required. Many microcomputers on the market meet his requirements and every day new developments are being introduced. Obviously the business machine required would be more expensive than some of the computers you had looked at but in some cases they were the same basic machine with larger memories and different backing store devices.

Most microcomputers use the byte as the basic unit of storage. The code to store this character consists of eight adjacent pieces of information. The information can be stored as 'charges' and 'no charges' on electronic devices, or it may be represented by a timed sequence of electronic pulses passing along a wire (Fig. 2.2). Each time interval may contain a high voltage 'pulse' or a low voltage 'no pulse'. An easy way to represent the two states which can occur is to represent one state as a '1' and the other as '0'. In this way we can write down the codes that represent the characters as strings of eight 1's and 0's.

Pulses

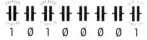

Charged Devices

Fig.2.2 **Binary patterns**

The number system which uses only 1 and 0 is the binary system, and the symbols used are called **binary digits**. This is usually shortened to BITs.

Many of the new computers coming on to the market use a larger unit of storage consisting of two bytes and because of this they are called 16-bit micros. These devices tend to be very much faster than the eight-bit micro and they also have the benefit of being able to use larger main memories than earlier machines. It was one of these machines that you finally bought, as it offered a very powerful computing package at a reasonable cost.

The backing store offered on the business machines that you looked at consisted of magnetic discs. These are available in a number of different sizes and styles. All have a number of things in common. At the heart of each system is a circular plate coated with a magnetic oxide material similar to that used on recording tape. This plate rotates at high speed in the disc drive and recording heads called read/write heads can move along a radius of the disc. The device controller can switch the heads on and off and move them with great precision. The result is that information can be recorded on to the disc in a series of circular tracks and each track is divided into numbered sectors (Fig. 2.3). One or two tracks are maintained by the machine as a directory or contents list for the disc. To recall a piece of information from the disc, the directory track is accessed and the number of the required sector is found. The read/write heads can then be positioned at the appropriate track and switched on when the first sector approaches. All of this is achieved in a fraction of a second and because the heads can go straight to the required information this is called **direct access**.

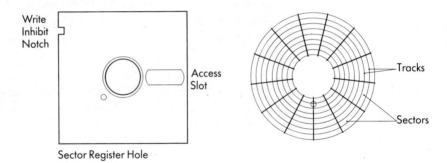

Fig. 2.3   A floppy disc

When John first saw a disc system he refused to believe any of this mainly because the disc was square. It was explained to him that the coated circular disc on this system is a thin plastic sheet. As the discs themselves are removable they get a lot of heavy handling as they are put in and taken out of the disc drives. In order to protect them and allow them to be used they are encased in tough plastic envelopes. Even so they are still fairly flexible, hence the name **floppy disc**. Various salesmen showed you systems with floppy discs, some with a single disc drive and others with two or even four. On some systems only one side of each disc could be recorded (single-sided discs); others allowed both sides to be used (double-sided). Two sizes of disc – $5\frac{1}{4}$ and 8 inch – are available but they are not interchangeable.

Each disc surface stores about 125 kilobytes of information and is capable of transferring information between itself and the processor at approximately 16 kilobytes per second. Obviously this varies greatly from one type of drive to another.

The most expensive types of disc drive available for microcomputers are called **Winchesters**. In these, the disc is made of an aluminium alloy; hence they are called hard discs. The disc is fixed on to the machine and in fact there may be more than one disc 'platter' on a machine. Each disc surface has its own read/write head which floats very close to the disc surface. The distance between the disc and the head is so small that a particle of dust getting between the two could completely destroy the disc; so the units are sealed and the discs cannot normally be removed. Hard disc systems have storage capacities ranging from 1 megabyte (1 million characters) upwards depending on how much money is available. The speed of transfer of data from hard discs is approximately 100 times faster than from floppy discs. The system which impressed you the most was one which had just come onto the market. This consisted of a removable $3\frac{1}{2}$ inch disc completely encased in a hard cover. When the disc is inserted into the drive, windows open in the cover to allow access for the read/write heads. Although smaller than the floppy discs the capacity of each of these small discs is in the region of 1 million characters (1 megabyte) and the hard cover would make it ideal for standing up to the type of use it is likely to get in an area such as the stores.

After a lot of heart and wallet searching you finally decided on a basic configuration for the type of machine that would be suitable. First it had to be from a proven manufacturer and to have a lot of software (programs) available for use on it. A sixteen-bit machine with a good quality keyboard as its input device would provide the processing power required. Output would be displayed on a high-quality video monitor which looked like a television screen but provided high-quality screen displays (Fig. 2.4). Backing storage would be handled by the new $3\frac{1}{2}$ inch disc drives. Several models fitting the bill were available and they were all nicely packaged with neat cases for processor and discs, separate keyboard connected by a cable to the processor and video monitor mounted on a tilt and swivel mechanism above the main case. This meant that all the units could be arranged for maximum user comfort.

John was feeling very pleased with himself after identifying his needs during his visits to the dealers, but you very quickly changed his mood when you asked him whether he had considered the type of printer he would need. He had completely overlooked the fact that while information displayed on a television screen is very useful while you are there to look at it, it is not much good if you want to send the information to somebody else. These are times when **hard copy** is needed and for that the processor must send the output to a printer. So off you went to the local dealer to ask about printers. Fortunately there was a very large range to choose from, but your particular choice was fairly simple. The dealer explained

Fig. 2.4 Westpool Motor's microcomputer

that where printers are concerned there are three main factors. These are speed, quality and price. The three things are inextricably linked; so if a high-speed printer is required it will be expensive. The higher the quality of print required, the more expensive, and so on. After some discussion you agreed with John that your particular requirement was for a medium-speed printer and that quality of print was not too important so long as it could be read. The dealer suggested that an inexpensive bi-directional matrix printer with tractor feed would probably fit the bill. John mumbled something about not wanting to plough fields with it and then asked him what he was talking about.

The dealer explained that when a processor wants to print something out it does not send it to the printer character by character but instead sends a block of characters. The printer has a memory called a **buffer** which contains these characters. As it prints it extracts characters from the buffer. When it reaches the end of a line instead of moving the print head back to the beginning of the line it advances the paper one line and prints as it moves backwards. So the print head prints in both forward and reverse direction, hence bi-directional, which speeds up the output.

The characters themselves are printed by means of the print head pushing a pattern of wires against a ribbon and on to the paper so that each character is made up of a series of dots. The wires on the print head are in the form of a grid or matrix (Fig. 2.5). Hence this type of printer is called a matrix printer.

The term tractor is used because the paper is fed through the machine on sprockets. It consists of one long sheet perforated horizontally into page lengths, and has holes down each side which engage on rotating sprockets and keep it in register. This drive gives a more positive feed than the typewriter style friction feed which is available on some other printers. The only restriction is that the continuous stationery must be used rather than normal A4 paper.

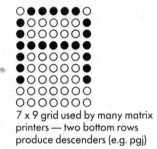

7 x 9 grid used by many matrix printers — two bottom rows produce descenders (e.g. pgj)

Fig.2.5 **A print head matrix**

John decides that this is definitely what he requires and adds it to his shopping list.

Assignment 3

John Jackson has a friend, Clive Turner, who owns a small engineering company and is thinking of buying a computer to help with his stock control. John is too busy to help out at the moment so he proposes you for the job. He wants you to have a look through all the catalogues and magazines available and find three machines which may be suitable and worth investigating further. Clive has no computing experience or knowledge whatsoever; so he is relying on you to guide him. He will need a description of each machine, the manufacturer's name and the model. You will then have to explain their features in plain English and say why you think that each machine is particularly suitable for Clive. At this stage it is only the hardware that is of interest. The information should be included in a written report which John can then pass on to Clive.

2.2 Software

During the time that you spent looking at hardware it became obvious to you that computers are really pretty stupid machines. Even the most 'intelligent' of them is incapable of doing anything at all unless it is given a set of instructions in a language that it can understand, and even the best of these languages is fairly restricted. These sets of instructions are, of course, the programs, which are collectively known as software.

John, ever watchful to ensure that he spent no more than absolutely necessary, wondered why so much software was required. You explained to him that two types of program are involved when running a computer system. The first is known as **systems software** and is required to enable the computer to communicate with humans at a reasonable level. This, coupled closely with the hardware, turns the box of electronic components into a multi-purpose tool. Of course, it would be possible to use the computer without pre-written software but this would mean communicating with the machine at its level (in machine code) and would involve keying in the strings of binary digits which would enable it to function. This would be extremely time-consuming and would require a great knowledge of how the system functions. The manufacturers would not be happy with this situation as the market for their machines would then be very limited. So they supply a number of programs that enable the machine to communicate at a higher level.

The main program supplied with computer systems is the operating system. It is usual to find that in microcomputer systems this program is permanently stored in the main memory of the machine in electronic storage devices called **ROM**. This stands for read-only-memory which can store programs but cannot be used for general purpose storage. As you explained to John, this is one reason why you recommended a machine with a large memory for his application. By the time the operating system and other systems software is installed there is significantly less memory left for the user to put his programs in.

John was impressed when you explained that the operating system would look after a number of tasks, such as allowing him to save or load programs with a single command. It can also handle a number of jobs that you very rarely think about and is generally very much taken for granted. Ensuring that sufficent memory is available before it loads programs, looking after the allocation of memory, allowing discs to be written to and transferring information to printers are all jobs looked after by the operating system, and they allow the user to concentrate on more important tasks.

John had assumed that all operating systems were standard (he read it in a book) and had paid little attention to them when you had been looking at hardware. Eventually it dawned on him that there were 'standard' operating systems but they were not used by all manufacturers, as some preferred to write their own. This might cause trouble in the future as it might be difficult to get software to be run by non-standard operating systems. It was decided that the machine he was to buy had to have one of the standards such as CP/M, MSDOS, UNIX or the equivalent.

Another piece of systems software that John was concerned about was the BASIC interpreter. When he found out that this translated programs written in the high-level computer language BASIC to the machine code language understood by the machine he said that he thought that it was a waste of money because he didn't want to write programs. It was explained to him that this was also built into the ROM of the machine and as such was effectively a permanent part of the memory. These devices which are permanently programmed are often called **firmware**. It was further suggested that a large proportion of the programs that he was likely to buy would be written in the high-level language and if he wanted his machine to 'understand' these programs then he had better have the interpreter.

Having finally convinced him that the software supplied with the machine was an integral part of the system it was then time to discuss other software, the programs to actually do the jobs for which he wanted the computer or the **applications software**. You discussed the possible alternative sources for these programs.

Basically there were three options open, and you had to try to give him some idea of the pros and cons of each supply. The first was quickly discounted because of the lack of time and expertise. This was for somebody within the company to write the programs required to handle the stock control. You could have done it, but it would have been a full-time job and when you suggested that another alternative might be for John to employ a programmer he shuddered at the thought. He had a point though because the company was really too small to have enough work to keep a programmer occupied full time, and once the stock control programs had been written he would have very little to do. Even when you pointed out that this was possibly the best way to get a set of programs to do exactly what he wanted and be able to change items within individual parts of the system as you required, it still did not seem a feasible suggestion.

A second possibility was to buy a standard applications package from a dealer 'off the shelf'. After all, that was one of the main reasons put forward for buying a machine with a 'standard' operating system. Lots of people produce sets of programs to help with the running of businesses and many of these programs are very good. John thought about this for a while and then asked how the people writing the program knew of the exact requirements of Westpool Motors. You indicated that this was a problem. The programmers write for a standard set of requirements and circumstances. Eventually the programs are recorded on floppy discs and instructions are produced to be sold as a complete package. These instructions or **documentation** consist of a number of sections, one of which explains how to set up the programs for use on your particular machine. Other sections describe the type of data that the programs will require and how to use the programs generally. John enquired whether this meant that the stock system might require changing to fit in with the program. You were not able to convince him that this would not be the case.

Obviously the programs will deal with the majority of cases, but changes in the way the company operates may be required as a result of using one of these packages. John did not seem too happy about this, but agreed to have a look at some application packages. After all he might be lucky and find one which exactly suited his needs.

He wanted to know what the third method of obtaining the software was. You suggested that one way of getting the necessary software was to get somebody to supply it as a **turnkey package** along with the machine. Then the software and hardware would match perfectly. This could be achieved by either getting a **software house** to write (possibly at great expense) the programs for the machine that you had chosen or by buying a standard package, installed on a machine and modified by the software house. It might be possible to get the supplier to make adjustments to the programs and tailor them more exactly to your needs. At least by doing it this way there would not be the problem of having to install the software yourself. You did not fancy the idea of spending a lot of time reading through detailed manuals and modifying programs so that they would run on a particular machine even if this only meant answering a number of questions asked by the program.

Having discussed the options available, you and John had to set off once more, doing the rounds of the suppliers and software houses to see if you could find either a turnkey package or an applications package and suitable hardware to do the required jobs. Eventually a company called International Systems and Software or I.S.a.S. was discovered. John thought at first that this might be a dead end but it proved to be very useful.

2.3   Installation and implementation

After a lot of discussion with Richard Sayle of I.S.a.S., John committed himself to buying a turnkey package. Richard agreed to supply a system which would perform the tasks outlined by John and would include all hardware and software required plus installation of the system and some training in how to use it. You were impressed by this very comprehensive package, as many dealers these days are content to push a system at you and then take the money. After that they are not interested unless they have to service it under the terms of the guarantee.

A service agreement was included in the package so that if you ever had any trouble with the system Richard would send somebody immediately to sort it out. Of course, all these extra details cost money but John could see the sense of paying for a reliable system. Richard gave you a brief run-down of it when the agreement was signed. He described the hardware configuration to you and told you the **memory map** layout. This indicated how the programs were organised in the main memory of the processor. Since any software which is running has to be resident in memory, it is important to make sure that programs do not interfere with each other. Of course, this is one of the tasks of the operating system, but that is itself a program and it has to ensure that it does not get mixed up with applications software. The memory is divided into blocks and the operating system makes sure that anything that requires memory is allocated to its own block (see Fig. 2.6).

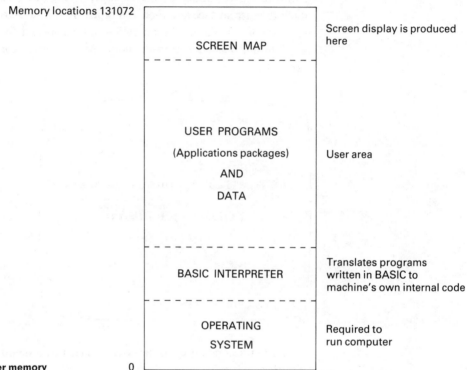

Memory locations 131072

SCREEN MAP — Screen display is produced here

USER PROGRAMS (Applications packages) AND DATA — User area

BASIC INTERPRETER — Translates programs written in BASIC to machine's own internal code

OPERATING SYSTEM — Required to run computer

0

Fig. 2.6   Computer memory

You recognise from the fact that the memory has an area for the screen map that the system uses a memory-mapped video system. Characters to be displayed on the output screen are pushed into the screen area of memory. The electronics dealing with the screen display scan that area of memory and pick up the characters and their position relative to the top left-hand corner of the screen. In other words, the screen map area is an exact electronic image of what appears on the screen. This can be useful for modifying screen displays or producing graphical output.

Some weeks later Richard turned up to deliver the system. He had made some minor modifications to the software and tailored the programs to your particular hardware configuration. Of course, you were aware that it would not be a case of taking the machines out of their boxes, connecting them up and then using them for stock control, but you were still surprised by how long it was to take you. The stores took on a very 'high tech' look when the processor was set up and connected to the printer, a demonstration disc was put in, and some programs to draw pictures were loaded and run, just to make sure that everything was working properly.

Richard took you through the operating procedures and showed you how to switch the system on. The operating system displayed a message to indicate that it was working. You put the disc with the programs on it into the drive, under Richard's supervision, being very careful not to touch the disc surface and then you typed 'RUN STOCK'. The disc drive whirred for a while as the operating system looked for the appropriate program and loaded it into memory. After a few seconds a customised screen displayed –

```
I. S. a. S. Ltd




      Westpool  Motor  Co.

      STOCK  CONTROL

         SYSTEM




Copyright ISaS 1985
```

After a few seconds this display was replaced by a menu giving a number of options –

```
              Stock Menu



      1.   Update file

      2.   Print re-order list

      3.   Print stock details

      4.   Utilities


Please enter required option –
```

The first three items were fairly obvious but Richard insisted on explaining them in great detail and said that if you ran into any trouble with them you could always contact him.

The last option puzzled you so you pressed the key marked '4' and the return key. Another menu appeared on the screen. There were more menus than Harrods' restaurant.

```
                    Utility Menu


     1.   Add records to stock file

     2.   Delete records from stock file

     3.   Adjust stock levels

     4.   Stock summary


Please enter password -
```

A password had been set by the programmer who produced the software and this **default** password could be used, but Richard explained that it would be far safer it you set your own password and then changed it at regular intervals. You wondered why a password was required anyway, but like so many things it became obvious once it was explained. This area of the program allowed major changes to be made to the **stock master file** which was the key to the whole stock control system. The last thing that you wanted was some unauthorised person having access to the file and changing it either maliciously or accidentally. Once the password has been set it can be given to those people who should have access to the master file, and the program will then keep everybody else out. Richard explained how the password can be changed. It only needs one line of the program to be retyped – but you have to know which line!

Having disposed of that little matter, Richard explained the current menu. The first item allowed new items to be added to the stock file. You were shaken to learn that all the information on the stock card index system would have to be transferred to the stock file before the system would be of any use. This should have occurred to you before but you had never given it a thought.

The second item allowed records to be deleted. This could be useful when you had sold out of an item which you were no longer going to stock.

The final options allowed for administrative procedures to change the actual stock levels on records to allow for 'shrinkage', and to print out a number of summaries to show the stock situation for a single item or group of items. These summaries could be useful in deciding on future stock levels. By referring to the reports frequently you would be able to see which items moved slowly and which were high turnover items. This should enable you to be far more efficient in the future and alter the safety stock levels and reorder quantities according to the speed with which items are sold.

Having spent a lot of time going through the running of the program in some depth, Richard then made some suggestions on the general running of the system.

First he suggested that you should copy all the program discs which had come with the system and you should always keep copies of any discs that you used. These copies should be kept in a suitable secure place away from the computer itself such as in the office safe. These **backup copies** of discs were necessary because the **working discs** might become damaged and unreadable to the machine. In any case, it was probable that the disc would wear out eventually, as magnetic materials tend to do, and the backups would then be required to ensure that any losses were kept to a minimum and you would be able to carry on running. The backup copies should never be used themselves for the day-to-day running of the system. Before any copies could be made, it was necessary to find out how to initialise discs. It is not possible for a disc drive to write on to a clean disc straight from the packaging; it must first be formatted for the system it is to be used on. Richard explained that all that you had to do was load a utility program from the disc provided. This program is called FORMAT and when it is run it asks you to put a clean disc into the second disc drive and press return. Nothing much seems to happen for a few seconds but in fact the program first tests the disc surface by writing over it and then reading the data back. If the surface records satisfactorily, the program goes on to set up the directory tracks and format the sectors for you. When this has been done the program tells you and asks if you want to format another disc. If you say 'no' then the program returns you to the operating system.

It was also suggested that the disc drives should be cleaned regularly with one of the cleaning kits on the market, as this would reduce the risk of disc failure.

When Richard had finished explaining how the program worked you were left with the system implementation to finish on your own. Obviously Richard would be there if any problems arose. After consulting John you decided on a plan of action. First the stock files would have to be set up to give details similar to those held on the record cards. Then the system would have to be tested to make sure it worked before the manual system was discarded. The best way to do this required the manual system and computerised systems to be run together, **parallel running**, and the results could be compared. This would also give an indication of the benefits, if any, to be gained from the use of the computer. Any problems could be sorted out during this phase and when John was finally satisfied that the system worked and could cope with every situation then the computer system could **go live**.

2.4 Setting up and evaluation

At the outset it was fairly obvious that a lot of work was needed to set up the electronic system. John realised that just setting up the stock files was a major task which you could not reasonably be expected to undertake. He knew, however, that Brenda was getting married soon, so he decided to have a quiet word about the extra work. He managed to persuade her that the overtime that was required to enter the stock details would all be paid for, and he promised her a nice bonus when the job was finished. Brenda calculated that by working late a couple of nights a week and putting in Saturday mornings it should be possible to get the job done quickly.

You had to spend an hour or so explaining to her how to switch on and run the program, which options to choose from the menus, and how the details should be entered. This was not really too difficult, as she already used a computer for word processing.

On selecting the option to add records to the file, the program asked for the name of the file. Since in the first instance this did not exist, it was necessary to make one up. It was decided that FMCSTOCK was probably adequate, and on typing this in the operating system checked the disc to see if this name already existed in the **directory** or list of files on the disc. The program required that a data disc be loaded into the second disc drive. As this had not been done, a message appeared on the screen, requesting a disc. A formatted floppy was inserted into drive 2 and the machine whirred away quite happily. The operating system was examining the disc to find a space for the file FMCSTOCK. Having found sufficient space (the disc being empty) it decided where to start the file and then made an entry in the directory. This gave the sector number of the start of the file, the name of the file and a type code. In this case the latter indicated that a data file was being created. All this information was necessary so that whenever this file is referenced in future the operating system will know that it exists and where to find it.

Having created the file, the program now requested some data to put into it. This data was transferred from the stock data cards to the magnetic disc with the following format:

ITEM CODE	DESCRIPTION	QTY ON HAND	RE-ORDER LEVEL	QTY	BIN NO.	LAST TRANS. ORDER			DATE REC'D
A 5622794	CON. ROD	35	10	50	32	050884	020484	100584	

character

field   field

record

When Brenda started to fill in the details after selecting the 'add to file' option and giving the name of the file, the program then asked for the input field by field.

First it asked for the item code to be input and, to Brenda's surprise if she made a mistake typing this value, the program then made the terminal bleep and displayed a message

INCORRECT ITEM CODE – PLEASE RETYPE

At first this seemed uncanny but you explained that each item code was created by Hotsun in a special way. This consisted of a letter to indicate the type of component; A for engine; B for transmission and so on. Following the letter is a two digit code which indicates the model for which the part is made and a four figure code to identify the particular component. The last digit is used to check that the previous digits are correct. Whenever an item code is typed into the computer part of the program carries out checks to **validate** it. First it is checked to make sure that it starts with a letter and has the correct number of characters. If either of these tests fails, the program will produce an **error message** on the screen. Assuming that the code has passed these tests the numeric part of the code is checked further. The final digit is removed and an arithmetic test is applied to the remaining digits. The answer obtained should be equal to the check digit.

For example

A	56	2279	4
Engine	Hotsun	Con. Rod	check
component	Supersport		digit

To validate this, the numeric portion has weights added

5	6	2	2	7	9		4	code
7	6	5	4	3	2		1	weights
35	36	10	8	21	18		4	code × weight

$$35 + 36 + 10 + 8 + 21 + 18 = 128$$
$$128/11 = 11 \text{ remainder } 7$$
$$11 - 7 = 4$$

The final value is the same as the check digit; so this code is correct. The value 11, chosen as the divisor, is purely arbitrary. Other companies use different values. If the remainder had been 1, an 'X' would be used as the check digit, and a remainder of zero would have given a zero check digit.

When this had been explained to Brenda she said that she had noticed the 'X' on some item codes and had often wondered about it. You explain that you have always had the opportunity to perform this type of checking of item codes but without the computer it is so time-consuming that it is not worth the bother. Since the computer performs the checks automatically and very quickly it is now worth using it to ensure that incorrect codes are not entered. You mention that the part of the program which enters data on to the file performs a number of other checks as well. It tests that reorder levels and quantities are positive and that they are between previously defined limits. In fact, as many checks as possible are built in to try to ensure that the data entered on to the files is 'correct'. Of course, if you say that we have three air filters in stock when we really only have two then the program can do nothing about that, but this is a genuine human error.

Assignment 4

1 Error checking and data validation is an important part of data processing. The speed with which computers process data makes this increasingly important. You need to ensure that any program that you buy has sufficient checks built in to ensure that as many errors as possible are trapped and the user is informed.

Make a list of as many checks as possible that you would like to see incorporated in the Westpool Motor Company's stock control system. For example if a date has to be entered you might like to check that the program would not accept the 31/6/85 as an entry.

2 John's friend Clive has now got to the stage where he requires help in buying software. John suggests that you produce a short report giving the possible sources of programs and the advantages and disadvantages of each source. Produce this document as a formal report to be passed on to Clive.

3 Using either a stock control program or a file management program set up a stock master file for the Westpool Motor Company using the information from Assignment 1. You will require the documentation for the system that you are using and your teacher may have to give some help and guidance. If a stock control package is not available, then VU-FILE or a similar package may be used.

4 Use the data from Table 2 of Assignment 1 to update your stock file.

Exercise 1

1   A firm owns a chain of shops and a warehouse to supply them; a computer is being used to control the flow and ordering of stock.

a) What files of data would have to be stored?

b) What type of output would need to be produced to help keep supplies in the shops and the warehouse at suitable levels?

c) What checks on the input data would be desirable?

(Oxford Board)

2   Each record in a stock master file consists of three fields: a key field, MK; a current stock level field, CSL; and a minimum stock level field, MSL.

All the key values are positive whole numbers and all records have distinct keys. The records are stored in ascending key order. The file is terminated by a dummy record with key -1.

The master file is updated at the end of each week so that the current stock level becomes the new stock level, NSL, using a transaction file which records the week's sales.

Each record in the transaction file consists of two fields: a key field, TK and a sales this week field, STW, which may be zero. There should be only one transaction record for each item in stock. The transaction records are arranged in ascending key order and the file is terminated by a dummy record with key -1.

Draw the flowchart for updating the master file and for the output of the key and the new stock level for any record where the new stock level is less than the minimum stock level.

(JMB)

2.5 Word processing

The present stage that you have reached with the stock control system is that of parallel running. The computer seems to be performing perfectly and you are getting a very efficient service. Soon you will be able to forget about constantly updating the stock cards and rely solely on the computer system. Every time something is taken out of stock you will be able to update the stock record by typing in the details to the appropriate option on the menu. At the end of each week you can select the option which prints the reorder list. The program then searches through the file and creates a reorder file containing details of all of the items where the quantity in stock is less than the minimum reorder level. A report can then be printed indicating the number to be ordered in each case.

The reorder report could be passed to Brenda so that she can deal with the ordering, but generally you like to check it first to make sure that it is worth ordering all the items on the list. Quite often, for example, your experience tells you that certain items which appear automatically on the list may not need ordering for another week or two because of circumstances which the computer cannot take into consideration (a holiday break coming up for example). When the order details have been worked out, the reorder report is passed on to Brenda for processing. This usually means using her word processing system to fill in the order details.

A word processor is a computer which runs a program taking two types of data. First text and characters may be entered and then instructions as to what is to be done with the text. The two types of data may be mixed so that data can be formatted as it is entered. In this way the system can be used to create written documents, letters, fill in forms, and a multitude of other uses.

John Jackson bought a word processing system some years ago and Brenda went on a two-day training course to learn how to use it. The system consists mainly of a single unit containing a screen, processor and two floppy disc drives. Connected to this by a cable is a large keyboard which has a number of dedicated keys to enable text to be moved around on the screen, the cursor to be moved, and a number of other tasks to be performed by single keystrokes. The final part of the system is a high quality daisy wheel printer similar in operation to the one attached to the stock control system. The main difference is that the print head on this printer actually has a type face. A central wheel has spokes protruding from it. At the end of each spoke is a type face character. As the printer operates, the wheel rotates and as the appropriate character passes the print position a hammer presses it through a ribbon and on to the paper. This is very similar to the operation of a conventional typewriter, and produces high quality print but at a slower rate than the matrix printer.

The floppy discs are used to store the word processing program and text which has previously been created. This text may be complete documents, blank forms or parts of documents.

To run the system, Brenda switches on and inserts the word processing disc into the master disc drive. On her system, this means that it automatically starts up as a word processor. This is called a **dedicated word processor** but most computers now have programs available to turn them into word processing systems.

Once the system has started Brenda has a number of choices. She can create a document and then edit it until she has removed all the typing errors and other mistakes. This document can then be saved on disc for future reference or it can be printed out. She can call up a document that she has previously saved and edit or print that. This is what she normally does with the order details. On disc she has saved blank order forms (skeletons). All she needs to do is to call up these forms and fill in the details. Her machine has an arithmetic facility which means that as she enters quantities and prices it can automatically perform the required calculations and enter the values in the appropriate areas of the forms.

You, of course have always been fascinated by the word processor and have taken every opportunity to use it when it was available. You are very impressed by the way you can type text on to the screen and then overtype to correct spelling mistakes. Words that are missed out can be inserted, or words can be deleted and the changes do not show in the final document.

Brenda is now quite an expert, and has found many ways of saving time with the machine. Letters that have to go out to different customers on a regular basis reminding them to pay their bills can be produced by changing the names and addresses on a previously stored draft of a standard letter. The customer thinks that he is getting a personal reminder.

Even producing new letters can be speeded up by the use of stored phrases and paragraphs. Text that is repeated in a number of letters or other documents can be stored on disc and then called up to be inserted in the current document using a couple of keys. Brenda said that this is called **boilerplating** and in some cases complete documents can be created with very little in the way of typing being required. Of course, word processing has become more common since Brenda got her machine. It is now possible to buy a whole range of different types of machine. When you were looking for a computer for the stores the salesmen demonstrated packages which would allow almost any computer to run word processing applications. The levels of sophistication varied, but most could handle the creation, storage, editing and printing of text. Many could perform to the same standard as Brenda's machine with facilities to store customer records giving details of names and addresses, credit limits and so on. These lists could then be sorted by the program into any required sequence. Entries could be selected from the list according to some criterion such as the district in which they are situated and the details from the records could be merged with a standard letter to produce personal letters automatically to pre-selected customers.

You have tried to persuade John to include a word processing package as part of the stores system but he suggested that the system Brenda had was sufficient for the needs of the company at the moment. Still you can work on him, and if you can put up a good enough argument for such a package you will be able to add it to the system later on.

In the meantime you have sufficient problems with the current system 'going live' in the near future. You are fairly confident that the system will be able to cope and that any problems would have shown themselves by now but mistakes or **bugs** in programs have a nasty habit of hiding themselves until the most inconvenient moment which is why the extensive testing program is so important.

As for the word processing you will have to be content, for the time being, with borrowing Brenda's machine when she isn't looking.

Assignment 5

1   Use a word processing system to produce a skeleton blank requisition form which could be used in the stores. This form should have the company heading and a title. A space should be available to fill in the name of the supplier of the goods and the date. There should then be columns for item codes, description, quantity and price. A box should be provided at the foot of the price column for the total. The foot of the form should have a space where it can be signed.

This form could then be used whenever you want Brenda to order something for the stores other than normal stock items. You may, for example require pens, pencils or other items of stationery.

2   You are managing to run the computer system quite well but you are aware that you are to be in the stores for a short time. Other people have taken an interest in the system but you can never be sure of having somebody who knows how to look after it all the time. You have decided that what is required is a procedures manual giving details of all of the routine processes that have to be carried out. This is totally separate from the operations manual which gives information on the day-to-day running of the system and explains how to enter data.

Use a word processing system to produce the procedures manual for Westpool Motors' computer system. You may have to refer to the operating instructions for your computer system to find out how to copy discs or files.

The information included in the manual should be broken down into weekly, monthly, yearly tasks (or other time intervals as you think appropriate) and will include details of discs that need copying and so on. Remember that the equipment needs to be cared for in other ways; screens and disc drives need cleaning periodically and printers need paper.

3   You are determined to get hold of a word processing package for the stores computer but this means making out a good case to John. Discuss the situation with your colleagues and then produce a set of notes which outline the arguments that you will use as the basis for negotiation. These notes should indicate the great benefits that will be gained by having another word processing system available to you, and should indicate the type of work which you believe the system can do.

Glossary

backing store   Extra permanent memory, external to the central processing unit, used to store programs and data.

BASIC   Programming language Beginners All-purpose Symbolic Instruction Code.

bit   Binary digit – a zero or a one.

boiler plating   Creating documents from pre-stored text using a word processor.

bug   Error in a program.

byte   The binary patterns used within the computer system to store a single character.

check digit   Value at end of code numbers which allows mathematical verification to be carried out.

documentation   Written information supplied with programs to explain how to use them and what they do.

error message   Information produced by program when a mistake has been made or a malfunction has occurred.

field   Data item.

firmware   Programs contained within read only memory.

file   Collection of related records.

floppy disc   Magnetic disc using thin plastic sheet as the base material. This is so flexible that it must be permanently housed in a thicker plastic envelope.

going live   Transferring completely to the user of a computer system after testing to make sure it works.

hard copy   Output printed on paper.

hard disc   Magnetic disc which uses a metal base material which is rigid. Available in a variety of different types – EDS FDS and Winchester.

hardware   Machines and equipment associated with computers.

integrated circuit   A device containing a number of electronic components etched on to the surface of a thin piece of silicon or gallium arsenide.

kilobyte   1024 bytes – a measure of the capacity or size of a computer system.

magnetic disc   Circular sheet of material coated with a magnetic oxide – used as backing store.

memory map   Indicates where each piece of software may be found in memory – shows layout of the memory.

operating system   Program to control the flow of information through the system.

parallel running   Using a computerised system alongside a manual one to compare the performance.

program   List of instructions, written in a language that the computer understands, enabling it to perform tasks.

RAM   Random access memory.

record   Collection of related fields.

ROM   Read only memory.

sector   Addressable part of magnetic disc.

self-checking code   Code number with check digit attached.

software   Programs used by computer system.

software house   Company specialising in writing programs for customers.

systems software   Programs enabling the computer to function.

turnkey package   System supplied as hardware and software to do a specific job.

two-state device   Any mechanism which has two stable states or conditions.

validate   Check that data obeys certain rules (that it is 'correct').

word processing   Application of computer to creation, editing and storing of text.

working discs   Discs in day-to-day use on the system.

3 Integrated business software

While you were looking at systems to install at Westpool Motors many of the salesmen you talked to suggested that what was required was a fully integrated system. You spent a lot of time discussing the advantages and disadvantages of such systems with John and with representatives of a number of companies before you actually went ahead with the purchase and installation of the stock control system.

3.1 A typical system

A number of software houses are producing systems that can handle most functions connected with the administration of small businesses. Some of these packages are available as applications packages to run on a number of microcomputers; others have been developed by computer manufacturers to run on their systems, and are sold as turnkey packages.

The philosophy is that a number of areas of business administration are linked together and many of them can be handled by computer programs. By selling a set (or suite) of programs to handle all these related tasks the computer can play a larger part in the administration of the business.

The accounting system touches on most functions in a company. It governs the financial dealings of the company and so must know which goods have been purchased and the amount to be paid. It must also know which goods have been sold and the payment expected, the value of the goods on the shelves and how much each employee should be paid. In this way, the accounting system is central to systems for buying and selling goods and paying wages.

Integrated business systems tend to have the **accounting system** as the main section and then add on to this programs to deal with **payroll, stock control, order processing, word processing** and **mailing list**. The computer is then given data from each of the individual systems and it produces whatever reports (invoices, orders, payslips etc.) are required and updates the relevant files. This can be as shown in Fig. 3.1.

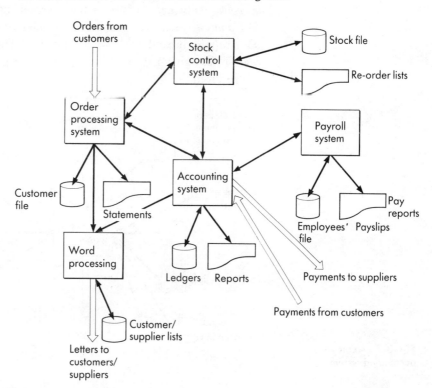

Fig. 3.1   An integrated business system

3.2   Accounting system

The accounting system (Fig. 3.2) is required to maintain three files: the **nominal ledger**, the **sales ledger** and the **purchase ledger**. These are stored on backing store (on floppy disc, for example) and contain all the financial information relating to the company. In addition it must be possible to recover information from these files and produce reports. Some of them will be required on a regular basis (to present end of year accounts, for example), others will be required at intervals to give information to management. The latter are called **ad hoc** reports and if they are to be useful they must contain the right sort of information. The **sales ledger** system holds details of all customer accounts and registers all sales transactions. A record is kept of the names, addresses, telephone numbers and credit limits of all the people who are allowed to buy from the firm on credit. Every time a customer buys something from you the details of the transaction are stored and can be used to produce details of goods supplied and the money owed to you. These details are printed in a number of ways *statements* – reports sent to customers giving details of goods supplied and payment received and outstanding;

day book – daily record of transactions carried out;

VAT analysis – details of transactions which require VAT to be paid;

sales analysis – breakdown of types of goods sold in a particular time period;

ledger cards – giving details of each customer's purchases and payments received.

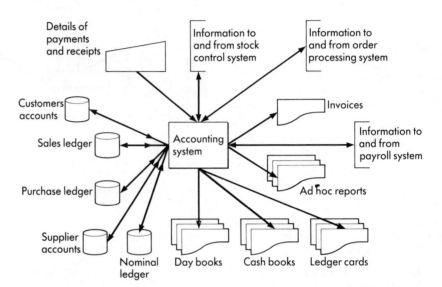

Fig. 3.2   A company accounting system

You consider that Westpool Motors would find this system very useful when dealing with credit customers – other garages in the area which buy Hotsun spares from you but less useful for cash customers buying spare parts over the counter.

The **purchase ledger** (Fig. 3.3) is a file which contains details of all of the items bought by the company and the money owed by it. Details of the suppliers' accounts are held on file with details of payments made. Once again, the information must be provided to enable management to keep track of how and where money is being spent. To this end the information provided by the purchase ledger system is also presented in a number of ways

day book – a daily record of purchases;

cash book – details of cash transactions;

VAT analysis – breakdown of VAT rated transactions (in certain circumstances VAT may be reclaimed);

purchase analysis – breakdown of purchases made within a given period;

ledger cards – summary of transactions.

It is necessary that both the sales ledger system and the purchase ledger system can deal with incomplete invoices and partial payments. If an item which has been ordered by a customer is out of stock, it must be possible to fulfil the remainder of the order and invoice for it without having to wait for the missing item to be supplied. The outstanding item would be supplied at a later date. Similarly it must be possible to accept payments for goods supplied either in full or in part payments. The better systems that you and John looked at would allow a payment to be registered either for a particular item on a given invoice or as a partial payment against

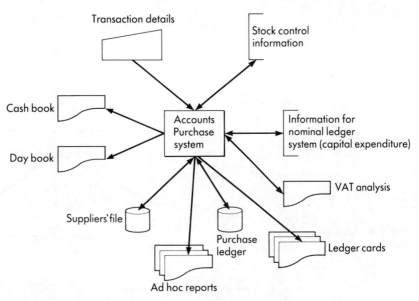

Fig. 3.3 **The purchase system**

the customer's outstanding balance. In other words the system could accept that every invoice would not be dealt with by a single payment in settlement.

The **nominal ledger** part of the system (Fig. 3.4) ties together the financial threads of the business. It contains details of the assets and liabilities of the company along with expenses and revenue. In any integrated system the nominal ledger will contain information drawn from both the sales and purchase ledgers. Details of accounts can be printed out along with ledger cards and various reports showing the financial standing of the company.

John was very impressed with the accounting packages which you looked at. Generally he felt that they tended to retain a lot of the flexibility of the manual accounting systems while taking a lot of the work out of maintaining the books. Even the names given to the files and reports were the same as in manual systems. He was also impressed by the way each of the systems had methods of correcting errors that might be made by operators keying in data at terminals. Obviously it is unreasonable to expect operators not to make mistakes and it was encouraging for him to see that any mistakes which were made were not the end of the world.

One thing which John realised very quickly was that the computer tended to present a 'black box' approach to accounting. Once the data was entered into the system it could only be brought back by the program and there was little physical evidence of the transaction having been made. You were one step ahead of him and realised that he was worried that somebody might relieve him of some of his money without him knowing about it

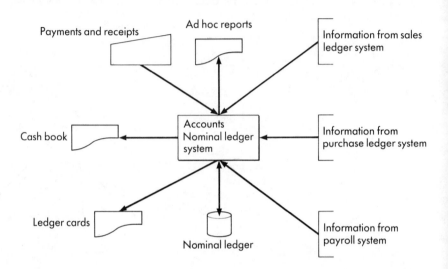

Fig. 3.4   The nominal ledger system

and you explained that all of the systems that you had looked at had the facility to produce an **audit trail**. This means that it is possible to follow through each transaction and print out all of the details relating to it. This would give, if necessary, the same details as would be available on a good manual accounting system.

3.3   Payroll system

The payment of employees often represents the greatest regular payment by a company. This is obviously related to the accounting system but in larger companies the payroll is often worked out by a separate 'wages department'. In a small company the bookkeeper responsible for the accounts usually doubles as wages clerk and is responsible for calculating wages, income tax deductions, National Health Insurance contributions. He or she would also keep the required tax records, update the ledgers, draw the money out of the bank and make up the wage packets. Extra complications may be caused by the fact that some employees may elect to have their wages paid directly into a bank account and others may wish to be paid in cash at the end of the week. Several different pay schemes may be in operation, some members of staff being on salary and paid monthly, others being paid weekly. At Westpool Motors, the car salesmen get commission on the sales that they make and any payroll system that is installed must take this into account.

Many of the integrated systems that you looked at actually allowed for a number of different pay schemes and also let the user define his own additions and deductions to take account of bonus payments and commission.

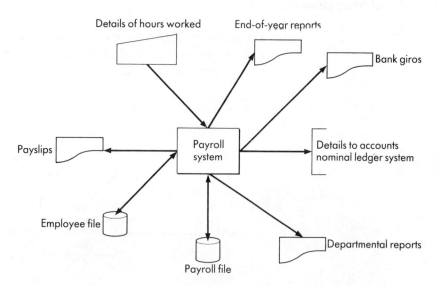

Fig. 3.5 A payroll system

Payroll (Fig. 3.5) was one of the earliest commercial uses of a computer system. By its very nature it involves carrying out a large number of fairly simple calculations according to predetermined rules on very large sets of data. The systems available are capable of working out the wages, making the necessary entries in the nominal ledger file, working out tax and other deductions and then printing the payslips. Other details must be stored to allow the employees and inland revenue to be supplied with details of tax paid at the end of the financial year.

Once the system has been set up and tailored to your own requirements by giving details of the pay rates, overtime rates, standard hours and design of the payslip required the user only has to enter the payroll number and the number of hours worked by each employee to enable the whole system to work. As this information is required for any payroll system, no extra work is involved in running a computerised payroll system. The end result, apart from updating the nominal ledger, is a payroll analysis report giving details of gross pay, net pay, tax and deductions on a departmental basis, along with printed payslips and bank cheques.

Having seen demonstrations of this type of system, John was convinced that, after the stores stock control system, payroll was definitely the next thing he wanted to use the computer for. At present Brenda has the task of working out the pay for the company, and although it is still a very small concern and she gets help from a lady who comes in part-time, it still takes the best part of two days to get all the pay details sorted out. If the company expands and takes on more people the part-time member of staff will have to become full-time just to make sure that everybody is paid on time.

3.4 Order processing

The nature of these comprehensive packages (Fig. 3.6) is such that most of the paperwork required in the completion of an order for a customer can be produced automatically.

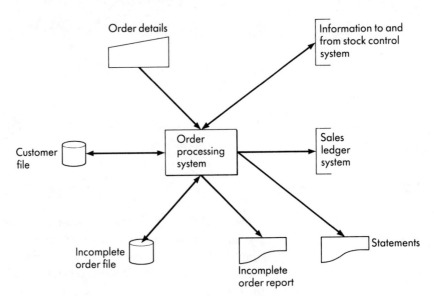

Fig. 3.6 An order processing system

On receipt of an order, the user selects the order processing section of the program and enters the order details (date, order number, items and quantities). The system can then check the **customer file** for credit details. If these are satisfactory (the customer's outstanding debts to you are less than the credit limit that has been allowed), the system can add the value of this order to the outstanding balance. Prices are obtained from the **stock file** so they do not have to be entered by the user and the details on the updated **customer file** can be used to send out a **statement of account** at the end of the month.

The **stock file** also contains present stock level; so the user of the system can be informed if any item is out of stock. Such items would not then be included in the present order, but recorded in an **incomplete orders file** and dealt with when stocks became available.

Details of complete orders can be **posted** (added to the file) in the **sales ledger** and the **stock file** can be updated. The system can then print out invoices and **delivery notes** with multiple copies where necessary. People who actually make up and dispatch the order can take the details from the dispatch note. They may even retain their own file copy of this document.

One person using the computer can carry out the whole order processing function. John was very impressed with this but, after much discussion with you, wondered whether it would be of great benefit to his particular company.

3.5 Stock control

In an attempt to produce a system to satisfy the needs of most businesses the software producers have included a number of other options.

Stock control systems (Fig. 3.7) such as the one you finally installed, may be included and linked to the accounting system, so that the value of the items in stock can be controlled. Reports linking the stock items to sales and purchases can give details of financial turnover in any given accounting period. Orders can be produced automatically when the stock level falls below minimum reorder level. At each stage, reports can be produced giving details of stock levels and orders produced.

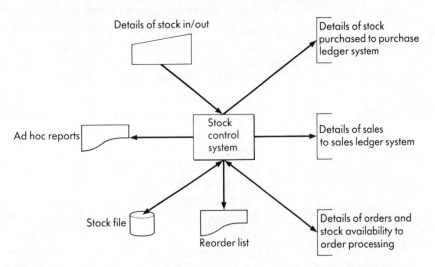

Fig. 3.7 A stock control system

On the office side, many of these systems included word processing packages. These are programs which turn any microcomputer into a word processing system. Linking in with this are mailing list systems enabling a file of names and addresses to be maintained. Letters can be produced and sent to any number of the people on the list automatically. Brenda's word processor is, of course, already capable of this type of operation and in general it performs word processing more efficiently than many of these packages, but it is incapable of doing anything else.

3.6 Why not an integrated system?

After visiting a number of suppliers of computer systems looking at the various systems and packages available, you discussed at great length with John the type of system required.

Having looked at microcomputer systems which performed a great number of tasks and some which performed very few, the final choice was very difficult. It would have been very nice to have bought a fully integrated system that was capable of dealing with every aspect of the business. John originally had visions of leaving the computer to it and spending his time on the golf course. However, a number of problems arose as a result of your discussions.

The first problem was that the system would have to be set up. Customer files would have to be created, stock files, ledgers, payroll details would have to be entered and payslips designed. Setting up the stock file on your eventual system was to be a big enough task without all these additional problems.

Of course not all these tasks would have to be done at once. It would be possible to introduce the system on a modular basis – say starting with a stock control system and then adding payroll and so on. Machine time would have to be carefully managed. If the programs were installed to run on a single machine which was designed to deal with all aspects of the business, a conflict of timing might arise. A tight schedule would have to be arranged to ensure that the invoice details were not scheduled to be entered when the payroll had to be run. If several people wanted access to information relating to their area of the business at the same time, problems would arise. It also occurred to you that if the computer developed a fault, nobody would be able to get access to any information until it was repaired.

The final arguments that put John off a fully integrated system were lack of experience and finance. He was worried about the size of the task and that he had had no previous computing experience. Furthermore, these systems were very much more expensive than the one he finally bought. He justified his purchase by saying that it was by way of an experiment. It would give him some of the experience that he required and if in the end the stock control system proved unworkable, it would not have cost him as much as the same result with a larger system.

When John discussed his requirements with ISaS they suggested that when he was ready to think of the next stage of development, probably computerising the payroll and accounts, they would be willing to look at a system which could be built on to the existing stock control system and eventually be developed into a full business system. In the meantime, John felt that he was happy to start with his stock control system and build it up later.

Assignment 6

1 John Jackson has given a number of reasons for not adopting a fully integrated business system for use in his company. Compile a list of advantages and disadvantages of such systems. Decide if he was right, in your opinion, to make the decision he did and then write a report on the problems of installing an integrated business system in an existing company.

2 If possible use a payroll package to produce the payslips for the employees listed in Table 3. You should also use the program to produce any reports which can be output by the system. Repeat this exercise for the two weeks' data given.

Table 3

Item			Employee payroll number		
	1354	2543	5643	1354	1432
Name	Helpfull B.	Panner S.	Fixit J.	Folds M.	Sellars C.
NHI No.	YR550913A	XY674356A	YR947568B	YZ572958C	YZ621486C
Dept.	office	w/shop	w/shop	w/shop	w/shop
Tax code	289H	240H	190H	240H	170H
Basic rate	190p	250p	280p	275p	150p
Basic hours	38	38	40	40	40
O/T rate	285p	375p	420p	412p	225p
Hrs. worked Wk 1.	38	40	40	42	41
Wk 2.	38	38	42	40	41

3 At certain times (usually at the end of the financial year) official forms have to be produced. These are known as P45, P60, P35 and P11. List the details to be found on these forms, say when they are produced and who they are intended for.

4 John's friend Clive is interested to see whether integrated business systems can be of benefit to him (despite John's warning). Use the computer magazines and catalogues to compile a list of systems available. You should, if possible, give some indication of the prices and the machines on which these packages will run.

5 John was impressed with the automated order processing systems that he looked at, but 'wondered whether they would be of great benefit to his particular company'.

Discuss this statement with the rest of your group and give reasons for why he might have come to his conclusion. What type (or types) of organisation do you think would particularly benefit from these order processing systems?

Exercise 2

1 A record in a weekly payroll transaction file consists of the following fields: employee number, department code, name, hours worked for each day.

For each of the following data items state one appropriate test which might be used to validate it

a) employee number
b) department code
c) name
d) hours worked for each day

(JMB)

2 A company uses its computer to work out the weekly wages of its hourly paid employees.

List the information about each employee which will be retained from week to week and the new data that will be required each week. Explain how the information will be organised and stored. Describe the operations needed to bring employee details up to date and produce payslips.

Glossary

accounts systems Set of programs and files recording the financial transactions and status of an organisation.

audit trail Method of producing all the details relating to financial transactions. Used to check that details are correctly recorded.

bank giro Method of credit transfer, i.e. transferring money from one bank account to another.

cash book Used for recording cash transactions – may be a real book or a report.

customer file File containing names and addresses of customers and details of previous orders placed.

daybook Used for recording transactions on a day-to-day basis – may be a real book or a report.

delivery note Document containing details of goods dispatched.

integrated system A set of programs with common files with data processing tasks in a small business.

invoice Document giving details of goods supplied and money owed in return.

ledger card List of transactions carried out – originally they were produced on card but may now be computer produced listings.

nominal ledger File containing details of organisation's assets and liabilities.

order processing The tasks required to be performed to fulfil an order for a customer – production of invoices and updating of sales ledger.

payroll system Set of programs and files used to calculate and keep records of payments made to employees.

payslip Document given to employees showing details of money earned and deductions from pay.

posting An entry in a ledger – hence to post an entry means to put an entry into a ledger.

purchase ledger File containing details of goods and services bought by an organisation.

report Any printed output from a computer system may be termed a report.

sales ledger File listing details of goods or services supplied to customers.

statement Details of transactions between a company and customer over a given time period (statement of account).

4 Data control and preparation in a multi-national company

4.1 Organisation of Hotsun Motors GB Ltd

Hotsun Motors, the company which makes the cars that Westpool Motors sell, recently celebrated the tenth birthday of the opening of its British subsidiary. The company is Japanese and while all the cars are manufactured in Japan many of them are sold in Europe. Hotsun GB is responsible for importing cars and spare parts for this market. John Jackson received an invitation to a birthday celebration at the Little Moulding-on-the-Marsh headquarters of the company. All the regional agents had been invited, and the festivities were to include a weekend in the luxurious Holiday Hotel, a visit to the company's head office in the UK and a champagne reception at which awards would be presented to the top dealers in the country. All this was to be at Hotsun's expense. Unfortunately John could not go as he had a previous engagement that weekend – so he passed the invitation on to you, and you went in his stead.

On arrival at the Hotsun headquarters, you were introduced to a number of senior members of staff. Over a buffet lunch you got to know a little about them.

Len Smart, one of the members of the group, turned out to be a senior **systems analyst** working in the data processing department. During the course of conversation you mentioned that you were interested in computing, and Len suggested that you might like to take the opportunity to have a close look at the facilities. As nothing had been planned for the afternoon and a number of the other guests were going shopping, you suggested that Len might show you the Hotsun computer.

Later that afternoon he picked you up from the hotel and drove you to the computer centre. On the way he explained that ten years ago when Hotsun were beginning to import cars they realised that they would have to organise a centre on which they could base the import of cars and spares, and from which a distribution network could be arranged. They took over a disused army camp which gave them plenty of space for storage, warehousing and offices. The parent company in Japan was already very computer orientated; so it was decided to install the computer from the start.

The company was set up with six divisions (Fig. 4.1), with the data processing division (Fig. 4.2) providing the information processing facilities for the remaining five. A large **mainframe** computer handles the actual processing, and all departments are linked to it, as indeed, is the parent company in Japan.

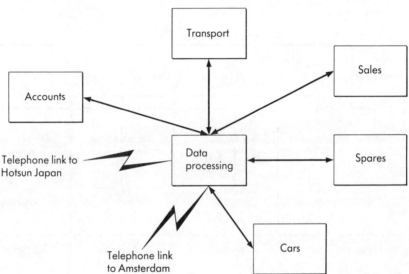

Fig. 4.1 The organisation of Hotsun GB Ltd

The accounts department is obviously responsible for dealing with the financial side of the company. Order processing, keeping ledgers up to date, payroll and financial planning are the main tasks that they use the computer for. In addition the problems of running multi-national companies were now so great that many of the accounts staff required their own microcomputers to run specialist programs and get immediate results – all to do with high finance and the exchange rates between the pound and the yen, not to mention the European currencies. Len promised that if there was time you could have a look at the accounting systems.

You had already had dealings with the spares department. These are the people who supply you with replacement parts for the stores of Westpool Motors. All the same, you were mildly surprised when Len told you that the warehouse covered several million square feet and housed spare parts worth twenty-five million pounds. Len explained that this department used the computer mainly for stock control. When you said that you were using a microcomputer for the same purpose Len smiled and suggested that the two systems were probably very similar but Hotsun's was probably slightly bigger.

The transport department began as a department responsible for ferrying new cars from the docks thirty miles away to a compound at headquarters where they were stored until sold. Over the years it had grown so that it now runs and maintains not only its transporters but also a fleet of vans for delivering parts, and several company cars.

HOTSUN GB LTD DATA PROCESSING DEPARTMENT

ORGANISATION CHART

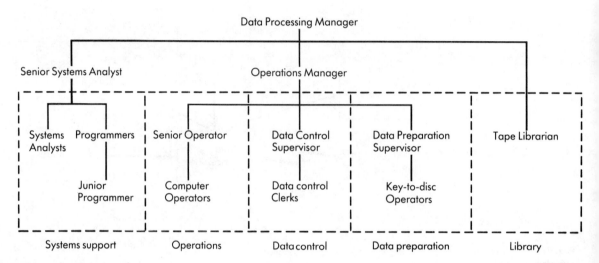

Fig. 4.2 Hotsun GB Ltd Data Processing Department personnel structure

You asked Len if this department also used the computer system and he replied that this was really his pet project. In the early days, he had been involved in setting up a **planned maintenance** system. Details of each vehicle in the fleet were held on magnetic disc. These records contained particulars of the vehicle type, registration number and service history. Details were also recorded of the maintenance required for each type of vehicle. By using the information from these files, it was possible for the computer to print out at the beginning of each week a list of servicing jobs which had to be carried out on particular cars or vans. The workshop foreman could then arrange for the work to be carried out and notify drivers of the times to bring their vehicles in. This resulted in a better flow of work through the workshops and vital servicing tasks were not forgotten.

All the cars imported are the property of the cars division. It receives the cars, stores them and is responsible for sending them out to dealers both in Britain and on the continent. It uses the computer to run a stock control system to keep track of the cars brought in and sent out. In addition, because a record is kept of the destination of every car, it is possible to use this system as a 'find a car' service. Suppose a customer walks in to a dealer in Manchester and says he would like a Hotsun Supersport but it must be a blue GL version. If the dealer does not have one in stock he can ring the cars division which will use a program on the computer to interrogate the file and find out if any garages in the Manchester area have taken delivery of the required model. In this way it is possible to supply the customer with his or her exact requirements.

The last division is sales, which is obviously interested in selling cars. Often this interest takes a number of different forms. The team of salesmen and promotional staff attends major exhibitions such as the Motor Show. They are also the people who run the highly successful Hotsun rally team. The computer is used to keep track of sales accounts; this is vitally important since the salesmen are paid by commission on the cars they sell. In this case, the salesmen are not really interested in selling single cars. They talk to fleet buyers and agents who buy dozens of cars at a time for sale or use by car hire companies and similar firms.

You were now approaching the entrance to the data processing department of Hotsun GB and Len just had time to say that this was divided into five sections: data control, data preparation, operations, library and systems support. With luck you should be able to see them all (Fig. 4.3).

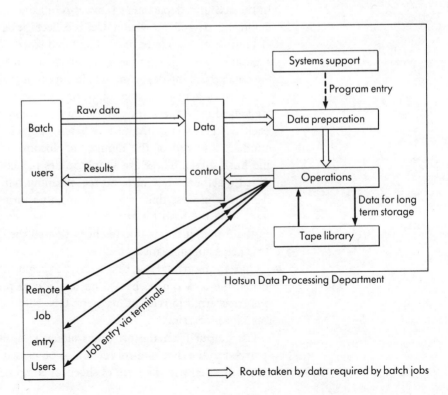

Fig. 4.3 **Hotsun Data Processing Department operational structure**

4.2 Data control

On entering the reception area the girl behind the counter turned from a **telex** machine and asked if you had been signed in. You were asked to sign the visitors book while the receptionist wrote your name on a lapel badge. Security was obviously very tight, and there was no way anybody could get in without being seen. Len used a card with a **magnetic stripe** to unlock the door to the rest of the department. Inside the door was an attractive open plan office area complete with the usual array of plants and shrubs in tubs. Len believed that they were supposed to make the working environment more attractive but added that they must cause problems for hay fever sufferers.

You were introduced to Ann Ditton who was working in one corner of the office. She was the data control supervisor and as such was in charge of the section. From what she said, it appeared that the data control section was the **interface** between many of the users and the computer. Generally people collected data within their own area and sent it to the data processing department. The data was processed and the information was either returned to them or they picked it up. The strange fact was that the majority of the users of the computer system never actually saw it. Ann illustrated this with a typical example.

The payroll system is something that affects everybody in the company. In the accounts department is a wages office which is responsible for producing the payroll but what it does is collect the data relating to the number of hours each employee has worked and so on. This data is recorded on a number of forms. These are then collected into batches and sent to the data processing department to be input into the payroll system.

A courier actually brings the forms across to data control where they are logged in. A clerk then takes the forms and carries out some checks. Each batch has attached to it a **batch control form** containing a batch number, a record of the number of documents in the batch, the date and **hash totals**. These are simply values picked out from the forms and added together. They have no real meaning but the program which will eventually process this data is set up to perform the same additions. By comparing the hash totals provided by the computer with those written on the forms, it is possible to check that all the data has been processed. This helps minimise mistakes.

Once the hash totals have been checked against those on the batch control forms, the data can be passed on to the data preparation section where it is transferred to reels of magnetic tape before going into the computer room for processing.

The output from the programs along with all of the original data is returned to the data control section to be passed back to the users. This output is usually in the form of sheets of computer output – what is called continuous stationery. This has to be checked for errors and the computer-generated hash totals have to be compared with the original ones. If any errors have occurred they must be corrected. Thankfully very few mistakes are made, and those that do slip through can often be traced and corrected after a telephone call to the wages office. Even so, this may mean repeating some of the processing. When the output is returned from the computer it may be in continuous lengths which have to be divided into pages and bound before they are of use. Fortunately the sheets are perforated in page lengths and there are machines which can split them and carry out binding operations. The printed payslips have to be cut from a continuous sheet, but again machines do most of the work. Eventually the bound reports giving various departmental pay details, a **cash analysis** giving details of the money required from the bank, and the payslips are ready to be returned. The wages office sends somebody over to collect its output, but some other users like to have their output returned to them. The finished job can then be logged out. So you see, the wages office is a major user of the computer, yet nobody from that section ever comes directly into contact with it.

The same thing can be said of most departments. Stock control sheets, details of car deliveries and various other data come into the office for processing and reports are sent back in return – the departments using the computer without actually seeing it. Ann often jokes with the people making deliveries, and tries to convince them that behind the locked doors they really have thousands of people with typewriters.

You asked if this was true of all departments, and the two Hotsun representatives shook their heads. It used to be so until a couple of years ago, but now many people are connected to the computer as **remote users**. For example, the accounts department enters all the order details through **visual display units** located in the department and connected by a cable or **land line** to the computer. Westpool Motors' orders for spare parts would be put on to the computer system in that way. Most of the offices were now using word processors many of which were connected to the main computer. You thanked Ann and then the pair of you moved on to the next open plan office area. You were about to follow a route similar to that of the payroll data you had just been discussing.

4.3   Data preparation

In this area a number of attractive girls were sitting behind visual display units. They were using the keyboards to enter data while the screens displayed the values input. Amanda Mass, the supervisor, brought you a coffee and while you perched on a corner of a desk she explained what was going on.

Each of the girls was apparently keying in the data for a job which had just been passed on from data control. However, you were surprised to learn that the data was not going on to the main computer but was being put on to a smaller machine. Although this was a **minicomputer** and many times more powerful than the one John Jackson had just bought, it was being used solely to prepare data for input to the main computer. Len explained that to key data directly on to the main machine tends to be a wasteful way to use it. Instead the data is keyed into a smaller machine, stored on magnetic disc and checked. Then it is transferred to magnetic tape which the large machine can read very quickly. In this way, some of the donkey work is removed from the main computer which can then get on with other jobs. This method of data entry is called **key-to-disc**.

Amanda explained that a number of jobs could be handled flexibly by this system and it was far better than the punched cards that it replaced. The program on the data entry computer could set up the screen so that it looked exactly like the documents the data was being read from. All the headings were printed on the screen and the cursor, the little block of light that indicated the print position, could be made to move automatically from box to box. This made keying in very quick, and it was easy to proof-read the data on the screen when you had finished, because it should look exactly the same as the original document. The program could also perform checks for **self-checking numbers** such as those on Hotsun item codes. If a girl made a mistake in keying in one of those, the program told her immediately, so that she could retype it. Similarly, hash totals could be calculated as the data was entered and this could be compared with the values written on the **source document** from which the data was being copied. Any discrepancy between the two would indicate that the girl had made a mistake and she could correct it immediately. Amanda said that with the old punch card systems the main method of checking for errors was **verification**. One girl punched the cards using a machine called a **card punch** and then handed the complete card pack and source documents on to a **verifier** operator. This girl repunched the same data on the same card pack and the machine compared the character codes in the card with those the girl was typing in. If the two disagreed, the keyboard locked up, indicating an error had occurred. The key-to-disc system could perform the same type of **verification**. Once a girl had entered the data for a job, she could pass the original documents on to her neighbour who could call up the original job. She could then enter a code which would indicate that she wanted to verify the entries and then type in the data. The program could then compare the second girl's data with that originally typed in and highlight any discrepancies.

All these checks meant that the majority of errors were found and corrected before the data was passed to the main computer. You suddenly thought of all of the newspaper headlines that you had read about computers making mistakes and wondered how it could happen after all the checks that can be carried out.

Assignment 7

1 Why do you think security is so important for a data processing department? Discuss this with your colleagues and draw up a list of reasons.

2 A recent article in a computing magazine said that while it was quite normal for the head of the accounts department of a large company to be promoted to the board of directors it was unusual for the head of the computing department. Can you make a case for the head of the data processing department of Hotsun GB being promoted to the board of directors should a vacancy exist?

3 You have followed the payroll data from the accounts department to the computer. A number of checks and procedures are carried out to make sure that errors are detected before they are processed. Compile a list of checks that have been or can be carried out.

4 Despite all the careful checking, mistakes do sometimes occur. Occasionally these are reported in the newspapers. Make a collection of such reports and discuss them with the rest of your group. Why is it that these mistakes have been thought worthy of newspaper articles?

5 A number of machines are used in the data control department of Hotsun GB Ltd. Among them are
  1) decollator
  2) burster
  3) programmable guillotine
  4) collator
Use magazines and catalogues to find out what these machines do.

6 A hash total is a value used to check that all the data in a batch has been processed. This value has no meaning other than in the checking context. A **control total** is used in a similar way but this value has some meaning. Consider a set of bills arriving at your house. To ensure that all the bills are paid and you do not miss any, you could add together all the digits of the dates on the bills. This value would be meaningless – a hash total. Alternatively, you could add together the bill totals. This represents the total amount you have to pay – a control total. As you pay the bills, you could add up the amounts paid, or the digits in the dates of the bills paid. When you run out of bills to pay you can compare your running totals with those calculated at the beginning. If they agree, you have paid all of the bills, if they don't you may have dropped one of the bills somewhere.

Can you suggest some suitable hash or control totals which could be used on the Westpool Motors stock records?

Exercise 3

Key-to-disc systems are being used increasingly for data preparation.
   a) Briefly describe a key-to-disc system.
   b) How might verification be carried out when data preparation used key-to-disc systems?

(JMB)

Glossary

batch control form   Form added to a set of documents, and giving some details about the data such as the number of documents in the batch. Used to help avoid losing data.

card punch   Device used to punch coded data on to punched cards. May refer to a data preparation device for transferring data from source documents to a computer system or an output device which punches data on to cards under computer control.

cash analysis   Report produced as part of a payroll system, and giving a detailed breakdown of the number of coins of each denomination required to make up all the pay packets.

continuous stationery   Paper used on high-speed printers. It is put on to the printer as one long sheet, perforated into page lengths. The computer prints on the pages which are then divided into individual sheets.

data control   Department responsible for receiving data for processing and ensuring that results are returned to the user.

data preparation   Department responsible for getting the data into a form suitable for input to the computer.

financial planning   Deciding how much money a system will require in the future and how changes in circumstances are likely to alter that requirement.

hash total   Sum of a set of data on an input document. The computer performs the calculation and produces the same sum. If the two agree, the probability of an error is reduced.

interface   A mechanism between two systems which allows them to communicate with each other.

key-to-disc   System for transferring data from source documents to magnetic disc and then to magnetic tape for input to the computer.

land line   Cable connecting peripheral devices to a processor.

magnetic stripe card   Card which contains data encoded in a strip of magnetic tape embedded in it (may be made of plastic).

mainframe   A large computer system with very large memory capacity and high number of peripheral devices.

open plan office   Office area where individual work spaces are separated from each other by low movable screens rather than fixed walls.

planned maintenance   A scheme for performing routine preventive maintenance tasks on equipment at regular predetermined intervals rather than waiting for something to go wrong.

remote users   Users of a computer system who enter data from a terminal situated somewhere other than in the computer room.

self-checking number   Code numbers which contain a calculated digit such that if the number is entered into a computer system incorrectly a program performing the calculation can detect the error.

source document   The document on which data is originally collected and recorded.

systems analyst   Person whose job is to look at how tasks are performed with a view to making systems more efficient.

telex   Communications system allowing text to be transmitted and received over telegraph links.

verification   The act of checking the transcription of data by retyping it and checking the second copy against the first. Where discrepancies occur the data can be checked.

verifier   Machine for checking the punching of data on to punched cards by allowing the data to be retyped. If the typing does not agree with the data punched on the card, the operator is notified.

5 Systems operation in a multi-national company

5.1 Operations

When moving on from data preparation you had to pass through another door which Len first had to unlock. The area you entered was very different to that from which you had come. It was still open plan but bright, noisy and stuffy. The tiled floor had ventilation ducts which blew out cool air and this was definitely what computer engineers called a **controlled environment**. The temperature and humidity were strictly monitored and controlled, and the air-conditioning system filtered the air. Len explained that this was necessary for the large computer system installed there (Fig. 5.1). Certainly Hotsun had enough computer equipment. The room was full of machines, each with its own fan and motor contributing to the

Fig. 5.1 A large computer installation

general noise. None of the machines seemed to be connected either to any other or to the power supply, but Len said that all the cables ran under the floor. The floor was elevated above the actual floor of the room to allow for cables and air-conditioning systems to be housed beneath it.

The equipment all looked new; so you were surprised when Len said that they were going to be installing a new machine in a few months' time. Not all the equipment would be changed, but an updated central processor would replace the ageing one used at present. The installation would be a mammoth task despite the fact that all the existing files and software would be completely compatible and run on the new machine.

This was something that manufacturers thought about quite a lot. People would be less inclined to buy their latest machines if it meant rewriting all the software and changing files. Even so, the new machine would have to be installed and tested. They would have to be certain of its reliability before they could use it for normal processing. The manufacturers would use the holiday period when it was quiet to carry out the installation work. Still, if any problems arose, it might mean Hotsun buying time on somebody else's computer to carry out vital processing.

You were, by this time, standing in the middle of a very large room full of equipment. While you realised that the actual layout of the computer was pretty much the same as a microcomputer system, you were a little lost. Len pointed out the central processing unit complete with the control unit, arithmetic and logic unit and ten megabytes of main memory. This actually occupied a cabinet approximately six feet high and twelve feet long in the middle of the floor. You tried to imagine how many of the Westpool microsystems you could fit into the same area but gave up. The thought of storing ten million characters was too much. The remaining machines in the room must be input, output or backing store was all you could think of to say. Len said that while that was true the equipment in the room was only part of the story. Some of the peripheral devices were actually connected to the computer room from outside.

Just at that moment the senior **computer operator**, Vince Dur, arrived from the depths of the room. The two other operators on the shift were at present in other parts of the building. One was collecting a new ribbon for one of the printers and the other one had gone to return some magnetic tapes to the **tape library**.

Vince typed some instructions on a VDU which was on a desk near where we were standing. This apparently was the driver's seat. It went by the name of **master console** but it was no more than a normal visual display unit. The computer however, tended to treat it as something special. It was used to start and stop the processor, select jobs for processing, and generally control the whole system. In response to Vince's instructions, the screen filled with information. The jobs that were being worked on at present were displayed along with information about those jobs. Suddenly the screen display changed and a message flashed up. Vince said that it indicated that a program which was running required data from a magnetic disc which was not on the system at present – he would have to go and change a disc. Len suggested that you should go along and have a look; so you walked through the room. Passing what appeared to be rows of six-foot high tape recorders, you arrived at a group of machines which looked like glass-topped dish washers.

There were eight of these disc drives in two groups of four. Vince walked over to one of the machines and pressed a button on the front. This took the unit **off-line** and allowed him to lift the Perspex lid. The disc pack (Fig. 5.2) looked like a pile of LP records although they were slightly

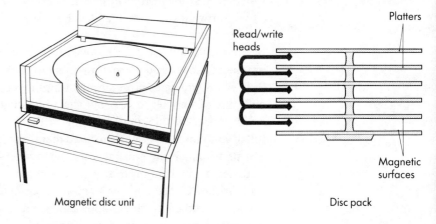

Fig.5.2 Magnetic disc unit and disc pack

Magnetic disc unit

Platters

Read/write heads

Magnetic surfaces

Disc pack

larger and brown in colour. Each disc was used to store programs and data in the same way that a floppy disc does, but these were **EDS (exchangeable disc system) packs**. Vince picked up a plastic cover from the top of one of the machines and placed it over the disc pack. The cover locked on to the central spindle, and with a flick of the wrist he pulled the enclosed pack off the machine. He quickly fastened a base on to the cover so that the discs were completely encased and free from contamination by dust.

The disc pack contained six separate discs on a central spindle. All the inner surfaces had the same magnetic coating as used on floppy discs; so there were ten recording surfaces. When in position on the disc drive unit, each surface had a read/write head associated with it. These travel in unison across the discs so close to the surface that a single speck of dust, or even a particle of smoke could become trapped between the heads and the surface and cause severe damage. This is why it so important to have the controlled environment and the protection for the discs themselves.

Information is stored on the discs on tracks in the same way as on floppy discs, the main difference being that because of the multiple surfaces available and the read/write heads moving together the tracks themselves form cylinders of information. Each disc could hold the region of 500 megabytes or 500,000,000 characters of data. Vince placed the disc he had removed on a rack and picked up another one. He examined a number printed on a sticky label on the side of the plastic case and then removed the base cover. Placing the pack on the free machine he flicked his wrist to release the lock and removed the cover. He brought down the lid of the disc drive and pressed a button to bring the machine **on line** again. This meant that the computer could now talk directly to the disc drive unit, and immediately the read/write heads emerged from the side of the machine and started moving in and out between the disc surfaces.

When you explained that you were familiar with floppy discs on a micro-computer system Vince said that they could not possibly cope with anything of such small capacity. The volume of data that the Hotsun machine processed was so large that they would be permanently changing discs if anything smaller than their present system was used. Just at that moment another operator came into the computer room. This turned out to be Alan Prentice, the junior operator on the shift. He had brought some magnetic tape files back from the library and now proceeded to mount them on the tape drives. Vince said that just as tape cassettes can be used for storage on home computer systems so recording tape can be used on large machines. It could be compared to the music industry. Recording studios use large reel-to-reel tape recorders for making master tapes of music because the quality of recording is good and it has to be able to withstand a lot of handling. The music you buy from the store to play at home is often recorded on cassette. The cassette machines are adequate for home use and the machines required to play them are cheaper than recording studio quality equipment. The same thing tends to happen in computing. Cassettes are adequate for recording software for home computers but something a little more substantial, giving better quality recordings is necessary for commercial use.

Alan walked over to one of the tape drives (Fig. 5.3) and pressed one of the buttons on the front. This caused the glass front to slide silently down from in front of the reels and gave access to load the new tape. Taking one of the reels of tape from its plastic storage box Alan unwound a short length of **leader**. He placed the reel on the empty spindle on one side of the machine and fed the end of tape into a slot. Pressing another button on the front of the machine caused the glass front to slide back into place, and the tape then threaded itself across the recording heads and on to the take-up spool on the opposite side of the machine. Vince said that nearly all of the tape machines had automatic tape threading these days and it really made the job much easier.

A gentle hiss came from the machine and two loops of tape were drawn by vacuum from the reels into chambers on each side of the tape deck.

You were surprised at this, because until now the machines had looked just like normal tape recorders. Alan explained that the loops performed two functions. First, low-pressure chambers acted like soft springs during starting and stopping. Each tape reel was driven by its own motor, and

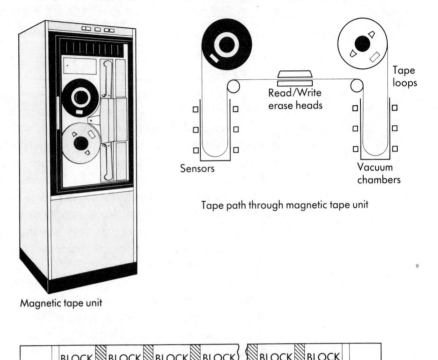

Magnetic tape unit

Tape path through magnetic tape unit

Fig. 5.3 Magnetic tape unit and organisation of data

Organisation of data on magnetic tape

if these did not start exactly together, it was possible that the tape might be pulled between them and stretch. This would distort the data recorded on the tape. Having loops in the tape means that if a delay does occur then all that happens is that one or both of the loops shorten. This brings us to the second reason, and that is that to make sure that the recording is of a high quality, nothing is ever written to, or read from the tape until it is running at exactly the right speed. This also means that both motors must be running at the correct speed. Sensors built into the sides of the vacuum chambers keep track of the lengths of the tape loops. If one loop gets longer or shorter than the other, the speed of the appropriate motor is altered. In this way, very precise control can be kept over the **tape speed**.

Incidentally, Vince said that as it actually takes a little while for the motor speeds to be synchronised and the **erase** heads are switched on during that time, a short section of blank tape is produced after each section or **block** of data has been written to the tape. These blank sections are called **inter-block gaps**. Len said that these can waste tape; so it was part of his job to try to help programmers to make the blocks of data large when they were to be put on to magnetic tape. You noticed a bin full of plastic rings next to the tape decks and asked what they were for. Len explained that they were called **write inhibit rings**. They could be fitted into grooves in the centre of the tape spools if the tape was to be written to. If the rings were removed they were **read only**. Tapes were generally stored without the rings, and this meant that a conscious effort had to be made to put the ring into the spool if necessary. This helped to avoid tapes being accidentally erased or overwritten.

One major question puzzled you as you looked at all the backing store devices in the room. Were they really necessary? Why, for example, were discs and tapes used? In answer to this, Len said that they were in business, and could not afford to buy equipment that was not necessary.

The disc units provide fast on-line storage facilities for data and programs. Also it is now common practice to look upon disc units as an extension of the main memory of a mainframe computer. By means of a system called **virtual memory** the **operating system** can 'pretend' that the discs are part of the central processor. The work carried out by the processor can then be divided into segments or pages. Pages containing information not required at any precise moment can then be stored on disc. When that information is required the current page is put on to disc and the new one is brought into memory. In this way, the processor can work on jobs requiring storage space many times that available in **main memory**. Len said that it was a bit like reading *War and Peace* but not having sufficient space for the whole book on the desk. If it was published in a loose leaf binder, it would be easy to take out the page you actually wanted and put that on your desk. When you had finished it you replaced it in the binder and took out the next page. You would still say that you were reading *War and Peace* even though at any one time you were only reading one page. The end result would be the same as if you had read the bound book. In computing terms, this system helps to make the system more efficient and increases the amount of work it is capable of doing.

'You would also see the need for so much equipment if you followed a job through the system', added Vince. It so happened that they were running the transport department's maintenance system at the time, and as Len had supervised the setting up of the system he was able to explain in great detail what was involved.

Each time a service or repair job is carried out on one of the vehicles, a job sheet (Fig. 5.4) is first filled in, giving details of the vehicle, type of attention it is getting, time taken, and so on. At the end of each week these sheets are sent to data control and then on to data preparation where the key-to-disc system is used to transfer the information on to magnetic tape. He pointed to a tape deck and said that this week's tape was actually on that drive. A few commands are typed on the console giving details of the job to be run. A control program or macro consisting of a number of commands then controls the running of the job.

```
JS1/TD
                          HOTSUN UK LTD

                       Transport Department

Job Sheet

To be completed for any work carried out on Hotsun vehicles.

Registration number [ ][ ][ ][ ][ ][ ]   Make_____   Model_____

Mileage [ ][ ][ ][ ][ ][ ]                         Date___/___/___

Work carried out:

    ROUTINE SERVICE

    New Vehicle [ ]                 Old Vehicle (pre-sale check)  [ ]

    5000 mile  [ ]      10000 mile [ ]          12000 mile        [ ]

    25000 mile [ ]      30000 mile [ ]          50000 mile        [ ]

    OTHER (please specify) _____

    ROUTINE REPLACEMENTS

    Tyres  Front [ ]                      Brake pads  Front       [ ]

           Rear  [ ]                                  Rear        [ ]

    Wiper Blades [ ]                          Exhaust system      [ ]

         Clutch  [ ]                      Other (please specify)_____


BREAKDOWN

Please explain the area of the fault (e.g Ignition failure)

_____

Please give details of parts replaced_____
```

Fig. 5.4 A job sheet

First (Fig. 5.5) a data validation program is called up and this reads the data file from the tape. Any records which pass the validation tests are transferred to a magnetic disc **transaction file**. If errors are detected in records, an **error report** is produced on the printer and the operators have to refer the data back to data control to sort them out. If that does happen, the processing is suspended and a message appears on the console to inform the operator of what is happening.

Assuming the data is correct, the valid transaction file is sorted by a program which uses the registration number as the **sort key**, and the resulting sorted transaction file is stored on magnetic disc.

The next part involves the majority of the processing and Len was obviously proud of his achievement. A program called the **update** was brought into the processor from disc, and it took data from the sorted transaction file and the **master file**, also held on disc. The master file contains all the details relating to vehicles owned and run by Hotsun stored in registration number order. The update program performed a number of tasks which can be best illustrated by the flowchart (Fig. 5.6). The

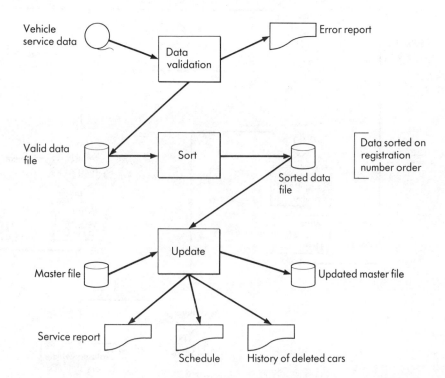

Fig.5.5 System flowchart for update

end result is an updated master file on which new vehicle records have been added and old ones deleted. A number of reports are also produced. One gives a summary of the service history of any deleted vehicles. Another report summarises the servicing work that has been carried out over the week, and the final one produces a list of vehicles that are due to have servicing carried out the following week. This enables a check to be kept, and also the work can be planned better from the workshop's point of view. Of course, not all the jobs carried out are routine. Job cards must also be filled out when breakdowns are repaired and this information must also be entered on to the system. Len was obviously satisfied that his system had improved the efficiency of the transport department.

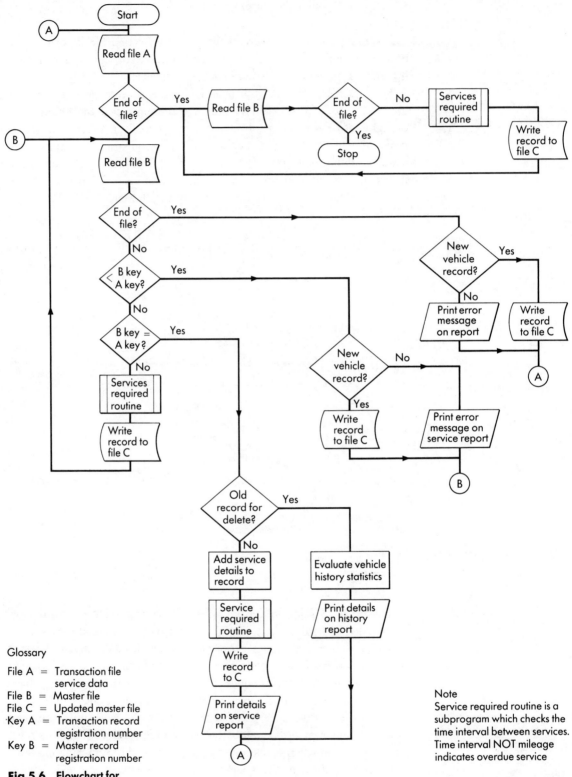

Fig.5.6 Flowchart for transport system

Glossary

File A = Transaction file service data
File B = Master file
File C = Updated master file
Key A = Transaction record registration number
Key B = Master record registration number

Note
Service required routine is a subprogram which checks the time interval between services. Time interval NOT mileage indicates overdue service

Just then a noise behind you attracted your attention, and you realised that it was a printer starting up to produce the service schedules for the following week. This printer was a fairly large affair and paper was being taken from a box on the front to re-emerge printed at the back at a very fast rate. Len explained that there was no point in having high-speed data processing capabilities if the resulting information took a long time

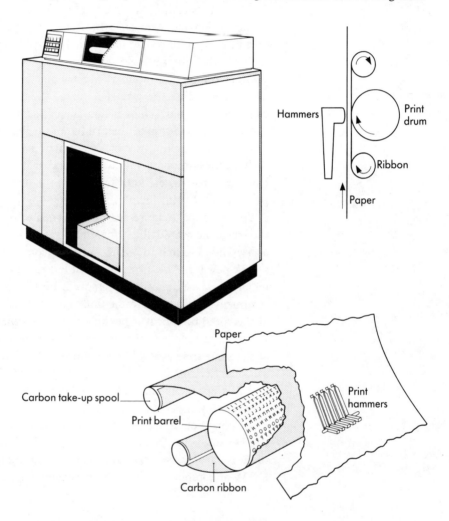

Fig. 5.7 **A line printer**

to be printed. Character printers were far too slow in this situation – these large printers produced a whole line of print at a time. They are generally known as line printers (Fig. 5.7).

The way they work is quite ingenious. Each character position on a line has the equivalent of its own print head. A hammer is positioned in front of the paper and a sheet of inked ribbon. Behind these, a horizontal print drum revolves on its axis. This drum has the typeface for each character position on it with each character in the printer's set repeated around the circumference of the drum. As the drum rotates, every possible character passes every possible print position, so the mechanism triggers the hammer to 'fire' as the appropriate character passes the position in which it is required. Each revolution of the drum results in a line of print being produced. As the drum rotates at 2000 revolutions per minute, this gives a high print speed. Unfortunately the faster it is driven the more uneven the printing becomes, as some characters are hit slightly before the proper print position and some slightly after it. The paper does not stop moving during the printing operation; so this type of printing is often known as 'hit on the run printing'.

Other printers on the market carry out the same type of printing, but in a slightly different way. On these, the print drum is replaced by a chain of print which moves horizontally across the paper, passes round sprockets at each side of the printer and is then joined up to form a continuous loop. Each character is repeated several times on the print chain with the most frequently used letters occurring the most often. Once again, hammers are triggered to 'fire' and print the characters in the correct position as the print chain passes.

You were quite impressed by the speed of these printers but Len said that what he would like Hotsun to get was a **laser** printer. This uses a laser light source to 'write' on the paper which then passes through an ink powder. The ink is attracted to the areas which have been written on and the excess powder is removed. Finally the ink is fixed by chemical treatment or heat to give the final output. Because the print is produced at the speed of light it is possible to get very high-quality output at 2000 pages per minute, and the laser printer can print form headings and boxes at the same time as it adds the information. This means that pre-printed stationery is not required. At present these machines are very expensive and it is not likely that Hotsun will get one until the price comes down considerably.

You mentioned that you had not yet seen the machine which produces the Hotsun price lists, so Len took you to a large machine at the back of the room. A very plain box housed a very ingenious system for producing **COM** or computer *output* on *microfiche* (Fig. 5.8). Inside was a device

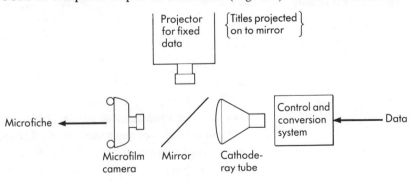

Fig. 5.8 System for producing COM

for generating the output and displaying it on a screen and a high-speed camera which photographed it. The film was then processed to produce the microfiche that is sent out to the customers. Len said that it was being used increasingly within Hotsun because the results required far less storage space than paper.

Time was getting short and there was still quite a bit to see, so after thanking the operators Len directed you out of the computer room and down a corridor to the comparative peace and quiet of a suite of offices.

Assignment 8

1 You were very interested in what was said about the system upgrade at Hotsun and it started you thinking about Westpool Motors. If you decided to upgrade your present machine what options would be open to you and how would you go about it? Discuss this problem with the rest of your group and make notes highlighting the problems likely to be encountered, possible solutions and the possible routes to increased processing capabilities.

2 The computer operators at Hotsun communicate with the computer in a language called **JCL** (job control language). This is the language that the operating system understands. All computers have operating systems of some kind, however elementary they may be. While you were talking to the operators at Hotsun they showed you the operator's manual containing all the JCL instructions. You have decided that a similar manual would be of use to you. This manual would contain the instructions that the operating system obeys and would include instructions for switching the print facility on and off, copying files, duplicating discs, listing directories and for executing any other procedures that will have to be carried out.

To create this manual you will have to extract the relevant information from the operator's handbook or instruction manual for your system — remember it is only operating system commands that are required.

Create this manual for your own system.

3 The figures mentioned for the capacity of the mainframe backing storage in terms of the number of characters held on magnetic disc and tape started you wondering about the comparative costs of hard disc and floppy disc. When you returned to the stores you decided to do some simple arithmetic.

Obtain a computer supplier's catalogue and get from it the prices of 16 megabyte hard disc packs. Calculate the cost of storing a single character on this disc. Carry out a similar calculation for the cost of a $5\frac{1}{4}$ inch double-sided double-density floppy disc capable of storing 275 kilobytes.

If you can get further information on prices, create a table giving the type of storage medium, capacity and price per byte of storage.

4 You were very interested in the transport system which you had looked at in some detail but one of the things which you were not able to see was a report giving the service records of vehicles deleted from the Hotsun system (because they had been sold off). Give details of what you would have expected that report to include (bearing in mind the information available to the system). Use the information to design a suitable output format.

5   You have been given the layout of a job sheet for the transport department's system and have been told that the data from those sheets has been transferred to the computer using the key-to-disc system. An extra stage is involved as the transport department does not send all the individual job sheets but instead transfers the data to an **input document** which contains the details taken from a number of job sheets at a time. This speeds up the input to the key-to-disc system and also allows some error checking to be carried out.

Design a suitable input document which could be used by Hotsun and shade in any fields which could be used as hash or control totals.

6   Draw a flowchart to show the stages involved in the subroutine called SERVICE REQUIRED (in Fig. 5.6). Note that this checks the TIME that has elapsed since the last service. New vehicles must be given their first service before they are 2 months old, even if they have not done the required number of miles. Similarly every vehicle is serviced every 4 months if it has not covered the required mileage beforehand.

Exercise 4

1   A particular microcomputer is advertised as having 16K ROM and 16K RAM, expandable to 48K.
   a) What is meant by K?
   b) Describe the differences between ROM and RAM.
   c) For what purposes might these two types of memory be used?

(JMB)

2   A certain magnetic disc unit has 11 discs.
   a) How many surfaces will have data recorded on them?
   b) Each surface has 100 tracks and each track is divided into 16 blocks.
How many blocks of data may be recorded on this disc pack?
Each block contains 1000 characters of data and the disc pack rotates at 100 revs per second.
   c) What is the maximum rate of data transfer to/from disc pack in characters per second?
   d) Give two reasons why the rate of transfer is often less in practice.
   e) Explain what is meant by a cylinder of storage and why data on discs is regarded as being organised in cylinders.

(EAEB)

3 a) Why is magnetic tape not driven directly by the reels on a tape drive?

b) Explain briefly how magnetic tape is driven by a tape drive.

c) Why are there gaps between blocks of data on a magnetic tape?

d) Why is the use of magnetic tape inappropriate for some computer applications?

e) A firm uses its computer to produce bills for customers, to handle an on-line stock control system, and process the monthly payroll. For each of these applications state, with reasons, whether magnetic tape is a suitable storage medium.

(Oxford)

Glossary

air-conditioning Equipment for maintaining a standard temperature and humidity.

block Set of data treated as a single unit. Usually refers to the unit of data to be transferred to a storage device or printer.

chain printer Printer which prints a line of text at a time. The typeface is linked in the form of a chain.

COM *Computer Output on Microfiche.*

computer operator Person who operates the computer by issuing commands in job control language.

controlled environment Area in which the temperature and humidity is kept constant.

drum printer Printer which produces a line of print at a time. The typeface is embossed on a revolving drum.

EDS *Exchangeable Disc System.*

error report List of records which have been found to contain errors.

inter block gap Blank space on magnetic tape between groups of records to allow for tape speeding up and slowing down.

job control language Set of instructions used to control the central processing unit.

key Part of a record used for sorting or searching a file.

line printer Any printer capable of producing text one line at a time.

magnetic tape Plastic tape with magnetic coating used to record data. The same material as that used to record sound.

master console VDU used to issue commands to the processor.

master file Main files in data processing systems, used to store the fixed data needed by the particular application.

megabyte   Usually used to refer to 1 million characters.

off-line   Situation when a device is not connected to the CPU.

on-line   Situation when a device is connected to the CPU.

operations   Name usually given to the department responsible for the day-to-day running of the computer system.

paging   System of dividing the total storage space available on the computer system into sections and then swapping these sections between main store and backing store as required.

peripheral   Devices which may be connected to the CPU (for input/output or storage).

sort key   Single field which is identified as the one on which a file may be ordered.

systems flowchart   Diagram which shows the flow of data through a system and the processing to be carried out on it.

tape leader   Strip of non-magnetic tape at the beginning of a tape spool which allows the tape to be loaded on to the machine.

tape library   Area, usually away from the main computer room, where tapes and discs may be safely stored when not in use.

transaction file   File containing the data relating to the latest changes in a system.

update   Process of using the transaction file to change the data on the master file and bring it up to date.

virtual memory   System which allows the backing store to be considered as an extension of the main memory, so allowing programs larger than the main memory size to run.

write inhibit ring   Plastic ring inserted into a groove in a reel of tape to allow it to be written to or erased. Without this ring the tape may only be read.

6 Software

Len took you to his office which was one of several in that part of the building. The area in general housed the section collectively known as **systems support** which consisted of systems analysts and programmers.

As you walked into the office, you mentioned that nothing had been said about the software that was being run on the system. Len said that a large system like theirs was capable of running a wide range of software, in a number of different ways and using several languages at the same time. To do this, it required a very complicated operating system to look after the throughput of jobs and make sure that maximum use was made of the expensive equipment.

Jobs are entered on to the system in a number of different ways. Most run on a regular basis and the programs are held on disc. The data required by these programs comes to the computer room via the key-to-disc system which you had already seen. These jobs are put into a **job queue** by the operators, and they make up the majority of day-to-day processing that is carried out. The jobs include payroll, details of car deliveries and producing service schedules for the transport department. This method of running jobs is called **batch processing** (Fig. 6.1). Other jobs are entered from terminals situated in other parts of the building, such as the accounts department where quite a lot of sales and purchase ledger data is entered directly using VDUs connected by cable to the computer room. This is called **remote job entry**, and the operators have little control over exactly what is happening when these users have access to the system; so the operating system has to be able to cope with this.

Any user on a remote terminal expects to be able to hold a conversation with the computer. This is often called the **conversational mode** of operating or **interactive** computing. What it means is that the operating system has to cope with two different types of job. Jobs in the batch queue have to be worked on until they are finished, but they do not need immediate attention; users on terminals, however, expect to get frequent responses from the computer and require a higher priority.

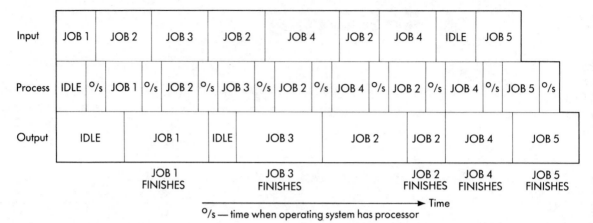

Fig. 6.1 Timing diagram
for batch of jobs in job queue

Fortunately the very nature of the computer system tends to keep difficulties to a minimum. The computer itself is incredibly fast and can carry out millions of instructions every second. However, the devices that it communicates with – printers, tape decks and disc drives – tend to be slow in relation to the processor itself. All these peripheral devices have memories called **buffers** built in to their controllers, and this enables the operating system of the computer to send a message to the disc controller device saying that information has to be transferred to a disc. The controller can then look after the actual transfer, passing blocks of data from the computer memory to its own buffer and then finally to the disc. This releases the processor to get on with another job. Transfers to the computer can be handled in a similar way, with the processor initiating the transfer and then getting on with other jobs while it is taking place. So far as the remote users are concerned, the operating system can rely on the fact that people are very slow to react to information. So several users can have access to the system at the same time. When a user types in some data or an instruction on the terminal it is sent down to the computer which responds as soon as it possibly can, because terminal users have high priority. A response is sent out from the computer and is printed on the screen, but provided that the response appears in a short time (2–10 seconds) the user is happy to think that he/she has sole use of the computer. In fact, in the time taken to respond to that user the computer may have also serviced several other remote users and carried out some background work as well. Such is the speed of the machine.

The operating system is the program that handles the initiation of the data transfers, decides what the processor is going to do next, makes sure that programs have sufficient memory and performs various other tasks. It must also make sure that it gets processor time as well. The simplest way to look at the operating system is compare it with a busy secretary.

She has some typing to do and a letter may be started on her typewriter while others in her in-tray await her attention. She switches on the coffee machine to make coffee and the telephone rings. The telephone is similar to the remote users, and she must respond to it immediately or the caller will ring off. The letters waiting to be typed are effectively the batch queue of jobs to be completed. As she answers the telephone it could be said that she is doing three jobs – making coffee, answering the telephone and typing the letters. In fact she only starts the process of coffee making, for the machine handles the rest and informs her when it has finished (this is similar to the processor starting a data transfer). She will keep going back to the letters throughout the day when there is nothing more urgent to do and so long as she finishes them in time for the evening post that is all that is required (in the same way as the operating system processes the batch jobs). Throughout the day she may carry out some filing, water the plants and tidy her desk (the operating system will also carry out housekeeping routines which have to be fitted in when nothing more urgent is being processed). The secretary may be disturbed from time to time to take dictation, make coffee or carry out other tasks with higher priority. In the same way, high priority jobs may be put on to the computer, and the operating system has to schedule them.

The main difference in the analogy between the secretary and the operating system is that the time unit for the secretary is the day, while that of the computer's operating system is thousandths of a second, and while the secretary may appear to work on several jobs at any one time the computer system may have to appear to be doing several hundred.

Len added that while this simple explanation was quite accurate it was a little distorted, since many modern computers tended to cheat and have several processors, so that several tasks could actually be carried out at the same time or **concurrently**, thus making the throughput of jobs even faster.

The discussion finally came round to computer languages. Len explained that the system was capable of running a number of different languages. As with the microcomputer, the processor worked in its own particular machine code but just as it was possible to have a program on the microcomputer to translate from BASIC to machine code, so similar translations were possible on the mainframe. On your micro at Westpool Motors the BASIC interpreter is held in read only memory, which generally means that you are limited to using the language BASIC if you ever want to write programs. On the mainframe computer at Hotsun a number of programs for translating from various languages to machine code are held on disc.

The obvious question that occurred to you was: why would you need more than one language? Len explained that first of all there were a number of different levels of communication within the system (Fig. 6.2). The lowest level was the machine's own internal machine code, which consists of strings of binary characters. To write programs in this language requires a lot of knowledge about the internal layout of the machine and how it works. It is also extremely time-consuming and fairly difficult, but it can produce programs which will work very quickly even by computing standards. As far as he knew, nobody at Hotsun actually used this language directly and it did seem to him to be a very old-fashioned way of using a computer.

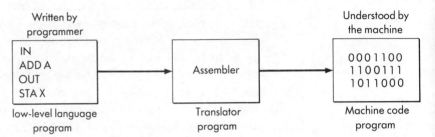

Fig. 6.2 Computer communication levels

At the next level are the **low-level languages**. They are very close to machine code but use words instead of binary strings. They are available on most computers but they still require a knowledge of how the machine works. The idea here is that each machine code instruction has words associated with it. These words or mnemonics make it easier for programmers to remember the instructions which have to be included in programs. It is far easier to remember the word ADD than a number consisting of a long string of zeros and ones. This makes the language a little closer to that used by people, but it takes it a stage away from that understood by the machine. Because of this, it is necessary to have on the computer system a program which will translate a low-level language program, written by a programmer to a machine code program which the machine will understand. Such a program is called an **assembler**.

Programs written in low-level languages will still run very quickly because the translation process is relatively simple because the two languages are so close to each other. However, writing the programs is still a fairly complex process.

Most programmers prefer to write programs in a **high-level language**. This is one which, like BASIC, is close to the language in which the programmer would normally think to solve problems. Each statement in such a language does require a number of machine code statements to enable it to work, and this means that a more substantial translation stage is required to convert the **source program** written by the programmer to the **object program** understood by the machine. This translation is carried out by a **compiler** or an **interpreter** (Fig. 6.3). Compilers are preferred because they translate the complete source program and produce as an end result, a runnable machine code version. This can be stored on disc as the working version, and because it has already been converted to machine code it will run very fast.

You understand the need for a number of different levels of languages but Len has still not explained to you why it is that so many languages are required.

'Well, it really goes back to my statement that high-level languages are close to language that the programmer would normally think in to solve a problem' was his reply. If a programmer is writing a commercial program which involves reading data from files, sorting it into order and

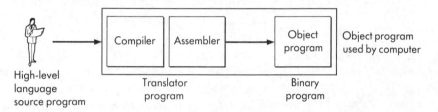

Fig. 6.3 Translation of a source program to an object program

High-level language source program

Compiler | Assembler

Translator program

Object program

Binary program

Object program used by computer

updating files, then he wants a language in which he can say something like: READ FILE A, SORT A ON ASCENDING KEY ACCOUNT-NUMBER, WRITE CUSTOMER RECORD. This is exactly what he can do in a language like **COBOL** which is the most commonly used commercial language in the world. For work of a more scientific nature he may require a language that can cope with complicated mathematical formulae, and in this case he may use **FORTRAN**. To get information quickly from files that are already in existence he may use a language like **RPG** which gets its name from *Report Program Generator* which is more a programming system than a language.

Of course, over the years, attempts have been made to produce single languages such as **PL1** (*Programming Language 1*), **APL** (*Advanced Programming Language*) which are capable of doing all the jobs required, but they have never really been as successful as the older languages. Perhaps this situation will change in the future but for the time being Hotsun continues to use a number of different languages, depending on the application. Some of the programs are now written in BASIC because it is a fairly simple language to use.

You asked whether the fact that Hotsun employed programmers meant that all the programs were designed and written by the company. Len replied that, as in any business, Hotsun tried to produce what it considered was the cheapest solution to any problem it might have. This meant that if software could be bought from a software house or computer manufacturer more cheaply than the company could produce it itself, then that is what Hotsun would do. One advantage of having the systems support team was that if bought-in software did not do exactly what it was required to do, then in many cases the software could be modified slightly or extra programs added to do specific jobs. A software house could design, test and sell a generalised package to a number of customers, each sale helping to cover the development costs. If the same package had to be produced from the start by one company, then that company would have to bear the full development cost. So unless the final product could be sold to other companies, the chances are that developing it would be more expensive than buying in. Many tasks performed by the computer do require specially written software, but a large part of the programmer's time is spent on what is called **software maintenance**. This means changing or rewriting sections of programs to meet changing needs or circumstances. A department may require an extra report to be generated or the parent company in Japan may decide that different documentation is to arrive with the cars and this entails extra data validation to be carried out. What appears to be a small change on a piece of paper in one department may require a lot of changes to programs.

Another obvious situation which requires major modifications to payroll programs is when changes are announced in income tax structures or methods of payment. Fortunately major changes are not made very often.

What this means to the programmers is that they spend a fair proportion of their time modifying somebody else's program. Each programmer may work on a number of jobs at a time and may be working with several computer languages. Len said that you might get a better indication of how the section worked if he went through the stages of a project with you.

Assignment 9

1 During your discussion with Len about high-level languages it was said that a translator program is required to change from high-level language to machine code. Most languages are translated by a program called a compiler but at Westpool Motors the language is translated by an interpreter. This works in a slightly different way from a compiler because it translates the program on a line by line basis rather than taking the whole program at one go. The end result of this type of translation is that a complete machine code version of your program (object program) is not produced. Every time the program is run it must be translated.

You happen to know that a BASIC COMPILER (BASIC) is available for the microcomputer but it will cost money. Prepare an argument that you could use to convince John Jackson that it would be beneficial to buy this compiler rather than continue using the Basic interpreter.

2 The Hotsun computer is used by a number of departments in different ways. Some use batch processing while others are using on-line terminals and timesharing. On your return you will have to explain these systems to John Jackson. Write out a brief description of how these two systems work and explain how it is that the operating system can allow this to happen.

Exercise 5

1 a) Distinguish between high- and low-level computer languages.

b) At a particular computer centre certain programs are written in a low-level language. Suggest why this might be so.

(JMB)

2 a) Explain the difference between systems software and application software.

b) Give two examples of systems software and describe their purpose.

c) Give two examples of currently used applications software and briefly describe their purpose.

(Cambridge)

3 In what way are high-level languages more convenient than low-level languages?

Why are low-level languages sometimes used, and for what type of applications?

For a named high-level language:

a) describe the character set

b) describe the rules for naming variables

c) write an assignment statement and describe its action

(Oxford)

Glossary

assembler A program which translates programs written in a low-level language to the machine's own internal machine code.

batch processing A method of using a computer by putting the jobs it is required to run into a *batch queue* and allowing the machine to work its way through them under the control of the operating system.

buffer A store which is used to collect data which is then sent, as a block, to a peripheral device.

compiler A program which translates programs written in a high-level computer language to machine code.

COBOL High-level computer language used for business applications (*CO*mmon *B*usiness *O*riented *L*anguage).

concurrent processing Using a computer system in such a way that it carries out several tasks simultaneously.

conversational mode Using a computer through a terminal to perform tasks. The user carries out direct communication with the machine.

FORTRAN   A scientific high-level language (*FOR*mula *TRAN*slator).

high-level language   A language close to that which the user would normally use to solve a specific problem. Each high-level language instruction requires translating into a sequence of machine code instructions before the computer can carry out the operations.

interpreter   A program which converts high-level language programs to machine code. Performs a similar task to a *computer*, but operates in a different way.

interactive processing   Method of using a computer where the user interacts with the machine or carries out a conversation with it. (See *conversational mode*.)

job queue   List of jobs or tasks to be performed by the computer. The operator sets up the job queue and the operating system decides the order in which the processor shall carry out the tasks. The jobs in the queue are said to be *batch processed*.

low-level language   A computer language which is very close to the computer's own machine code. Each low-level language instruction has its own direct machine code equivalent.

machine code   The internal set of commands which the processor understands. These may be a set of binary instructions.

object program   Machine code program produced as a result of translating a program written in either a high- or low-level language. This is the program which the system runs to carry out applications.

remote job entry   Method of using a computer by sending data to the processor from a terminal device situated away from the computer room. The job will usually be submitted to a job queue.

software maintenance   Modifying existing software to meet changing demands or circumstances or to remove errors which have been discovered during the running of the program.

source program   Program written in either a high or low-level language which must be translated by an assembler, compiler or an interpreter to become an OBJECT PROGRAM which the machine can run.

systems support   Department responsible for supplying and maintaining the applications software.

7 Systems support and communication

7.1 System development

Len arranged for coffee to be brought to the office and then settled into a chair behind his large desk. He started by explaining that the systems support section was run by the senior systems analyst who was directly responsible to the data processing manager. Its function is to provide software support for the computer operations section and service other departments' requests for data processing systems.

The usual procedure is as follows (Fig. 7.1). Whenever a department has a request for some information that can be obtained from the computer, or has a data processing situation that seems unsatisfactory, the departmental head gets in touch with the senior systems analyst. If the project seems worth while, it goes on to a request list.

When the request arrives at the top, a systems analyst is assigned to it. He will discuss the project with the head of department and together they will draw up the terms of reference. Invariably the department concerned will say that it wants the system improved without upsetting anybody and at minimum cost, and it required it yesterday. After some discussion, a compromise will be reached, the framework for the project will be written up, and reports submitted. These terms of reference will include an idea of the scope of the project, areas to be investigated and so on.

Once accepted, the project can start in earnest. The first part is an examination and analysis of any existing system or information flow. Basically you cannot improve a system unless you know how the existing system works. Similarly you cannot be sure of producing the correct information unless you know who requires it and why. This analysis is quite complicated and requires that everybody involved in the existing system is interviewed. Jobs are studied carefully to see how they are carried out, and copies of documents are taken to be analysed. This stage calls for tact and the

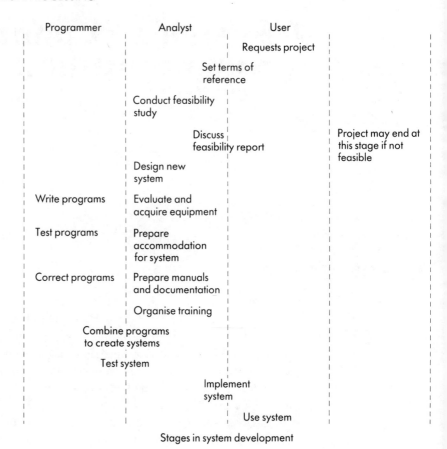

Stages in system development

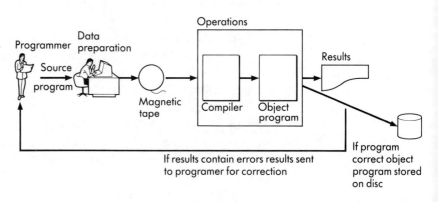

Stages in program writing

Fig. 7.1 Stages in system development and program writing

ability to get on well with people. When you start talking to them in great detail about how they do their jobs they tend to get a little suspicious, and you have to be very careful to reassure them. After analysing the results of the survey the new system is designed and a feasibility report is produced which gives a broad outline of how the system will work.

The report is then submitted to the head of the appropriate department and further negotiations follow. At this stage, the analyst has to sell his sytem to the department which will use it and the department in turn has to try to ensure that the system will do all that is required.

When the outline design has been approved, the detailed design work has to be started. The requisite forms and documents have to be designed to ensure that the correct data is supplied and the information produced is returned. The specifications for the file structures have to be written up and the programs have to be designed. At this stage, the analyst may well be part of a team which will include one or two programmers. This project team will be involved in producing the whole system, testing it and finally handing it over to the user. The programmers will write the programs on to forms called **coding sheets**, working from the analyst's designs. After careful checking, these source programs will be passed to the operations section where they may well be treated like any other batch job. In other words, data control will book them in and pass them to data preparation where they will be entered through the key-to-disc system and eventually passed to operations on a reel of magnetic tape. They will be scheduled to run on the mainframe computer as part of the batch. The operating system will bring in the program, call up the appropriate compiler from disc and then start the translation process. If the program contains errors, it will be returned to the programmer with an error list and he will have to make corrections before submitting it again. This usually takes some time as nearly all programs contain errors the first few times through.

Eventually the program will compile error free but this does not mean that it is correct. All it means is that the computer can understand the language used. The project team must now design test data to make sure that the program does what it was supposed to. Designing this data is quite a major task because the program must be shown to work for a large range of circumstances, even those which are extremely unlikely to occur during normal running. A number of files may have to be created containing data to cover all eventualities.

This testing again tends to be very time-consuming and of course every time the program fails it must be rewritten to ensure that it will produce the correct result when it is finally used.

A major project may require many programs to be written and may involve a large number of test files. A number of programmers may be involved, each writing a number of programs which will eventually be put together to run as a single job.

While the programming is being done the analyst has to supervise the writing and testing procedures. Modifications may have to be made to the specifications as a result of the test procedures. The analyst also has to produce all the documentation for the final project. This involves writing user guides and manuals ensuring that the forms are ready so that data can be input. He/she may also be involved with arranging for the training of staff who will be using the system when it is complete.

Once all the parts of the system have been tested it may be necessary to set up the actual work files to be used by the system if they do not already exist.

Finally, the system has to be implemented and tested to the user's satisfaction. The method of doing this is exactly the same as that adopted at Westpool Motors: by running the new system parallel to the old one if this is feasible. If the system is entirely new, this may not be possible; in that case a decision has to be made at some point as to when the users should **go live** and rely on the information provided by the computer.

At this stage, the analyst and the rest of the project team may well be looking for the next job to start.

You asked what Len was then working on, and he replied that he was heading a team responsible for setting up the on-line ordering system for spare parts. No doubt you would be involved in it at some time in the future, he said. Basically the system would give all the regional dealers a terminal linked by telephone to the Hotsun computer centre. Orders for parts could then be keyed in to the terminal; a program would receive them, and carry out some data validation to ensure that the keying in was correct. The program would then be able to interrogate the Hotsun stock files to ensure that items were in stock and immediate confirmation of the order could be given to the customer. Stock files could be updated as stock was issued and orders could be printed on a terminal in the warehouse. The staff there could then make up the order and dispatch it. At the same time details of the order could be printed out and sent over to the accounts department so that they could arrange for payment.

The present stage of the project (Fig. 7.2) is that a lot of the design work has been completed and negotiations are going ahead for the purchase of equipment. Terminals have to be bought for installation at the dealers. It is not sufficient just to put in a terminal though. Equipment is required to allow the terminal to communicate over the telephone network. Basically the terminal will be plugged in to a box called a **modem** which is itself connected to the telephone. Signals produced when keys are pressed at the terminal are converted by the modem to audio signals which can be passed along the telephone wires. At the Hotsun end, another modem converts the signal back to that produced by the terminal. The same thing happens in the opposite direction when the Hotsun computer sends information to the terminal.

An additional problem is created at the Hotsun end of the line by the fact that a large number of dealers will be connected to the computer. Although the machine is a fairly large one, there is a limit to the number of devices it can talk to at any one time. This is because each device requires a line or a channel which carries communications between the processor and the device. Many available channels are used by printers and terminals within the company itself. It is not possible to allocate each dealer a direct line straight into the processor. Fortunately not all the dealers will require access to the system at the same time; so it is possible to use a device called a **multiplexor** which allows a line into the computer to be shared by a number of users.

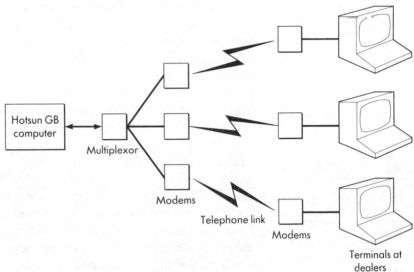

Fig.7.2 **The Hotsun on-line order processing**

The telecommunications equipment used by this system is very sophisticated and the dealers should be able to dial a given number and be assigned a line. If all the lines are in use a message will ask the dealer to try again later.

Until very recently, all the hardware for this system would have been rented from British Telecom, but now several companies are making and selling systems capable of carrying out the required tasks.

The telecommunications network is not entirely new to Hotsun. For some time, the various national headquarters have been linked together. Apart from the obvious telephone links, the computer systems have been networked to allow data to be passed from one system to another. Details of car shipments from Japan are printed out by the system in the UK, having been transmitted over the telephone network by the computer in Japan. Parts orders and accounting information can equally well be sent direct from the Hotsun UK computer to any of the other computer systems used by the corporation.

7.2 Electronic office systems

In any large multinational company it is inevitable that a lot of paperwork is generated: letters to customers, invoices, advertising and promotional information, customs and shipping documents and internal administrative documents. To help with all this paperwork word processors are used. You explained to Len that you were familiar with the word processor. Len explained that here word processing had been taken a good deal further than the small stand-alone office machine.

All the word processors could not only work on their own with documents being created and stored by the operators on floppy discs, but they could also be connected to the mainframe computer. The backing store of this computer could be considered by the word processing staff to be a massive electronic filing cabinet. This gave a number of extra benefits.

Each operator could file any document created under a number of different headings and would have complete control of how those files were organised. When information has to be retrieved the power of the computer can be used to search through the filing system for the particular documents that are required. In addition, the system can maintain a document keyword index, so that if an enquiry is made concerning a single piece of information it can quickly find all of the documents containing references to that item.

Suppose, for example, that the customs people at the docks want to check the details of a particular shipment of cars. An enquiry on the system for details concerning an engine number, import document or any other single detail relating to that shipment will result in a list containing the names of all of the documents relating to that shipment. It is then possible to recall any or all of these documents for examination.

You were very impressed but the explanation had only just started. Len switched on his VDU which was on a small table in the corner of the room. Until then you had failed to notice that it even existed. He punched in his identification number and followed that with a number of lines of text which the computer responded to. This took a few seconds, and then he said that every organisation has information which all employees should know and some that they may like to know. An extension of the word processing system allowed a common area that anybody with access to a terminal (and that was most people) could get access to. He demonstrated this **bookshelf** area by producing a list of items on the screen. Documents produced by the word processor operators are generally very secure and can only be accessed by people with the correct password. Usually this means the operators themselves and their supervisors. The items on the screen related to items such as general procedures, regulations governing the claiming of statutory sick pay and so on, which anybody could get access to. Putting these things on to the computer system reduced the amount of paper that had to be circulated and stored.

Of course, other items invariably get added to the list, and he selected an item listed as 'Jenny'. The screen changed to display a message congratulating Jenny Flynn from the accounts department who had recently got married. Len said that the system was often used as a sort of **bulletin board** for messages, and so long as these messages were kept short and did not interfere with the work of the company, nobody minded. In fact it helped to maintain a friendly atmosphere and keep everybody in touch with what was happening.

The fact that a bulletin board could be maintained illustrated another side of this office system. All the terminals were connected to a central computer where word processed documents are stored. A natural extension to the system was to allow the documents to be sent directly to the person they were intended for without the need to print them out first. You were not quite in step with Len at this stage, so he gave you an example.

Producing the feasibility report for the on-line ordering system required a lot of paperwork. Eventually this was pulled together to produce a draft report which Len had written up at home. This was then passed to a secretary who typed it up using the word processing system. Instead of getting that report printed out and then passing it to Len for checking, it was sent to his electronic office user area on the computer. He then logged on to the computer and called up the report for examination on the screen. It was even possible for him to make alterations to the text there and then (although he admitted that if major changes had been required he would have asked his secretary to do them). When the wording of the draft report was to his liking he could send it back to his secretary simply by pressing a few buttons. If everybody who required a copy of that report had access to a terminal he could have sent the report electronically to all concerned. Unfortunately this was not the case, so it was necessary to ask his secretary to have the report printed, bound and then distributed to the relevant people.

The same system can be used to send messages to people in other offices or those in other parts of the company, and the nice thing about this **electronic mail** is that it is sent to your area on the computer system and not to your desk. Len added that if he went to the Amsterdam office he could still read any documents or electronic mail that had been sent to him at the UK office. All he would do is 'borrow' a terminal in the Amsterdam office and key in his identity code. Any messages that have been sent to him will be displayed on the screen, and if necessary he can send replies. Similarly, if he finds that he has forgotten to take a document with him and it is on his area he can call it up from Amsterdam and have it printed out. The linking of all the Hotsun computers on a network means that increasing use is made of electronic mail. Documents can be typed on a word processor and sent electronically over the telephone network from country to country far quicker than the postal system can manage.

You are quite impressed by this system but say that it is all well and good for the people and organisations connected to the Hotsun computer system, but obviously they communicate with others not on electronic mail systems. It had to be agreed that a large number of letters had to be sent, and telephone calls still had to be made in the conventional way but it was early days yet! Improvements had already been made with the old-fashioned **telex** system.

7.3 Telex

Originally a telex operator had been employed to type messages on a telex machine, which is rather like an electronic typewriter, but it only has capital letters and is connected to the telephone system. These messages are transmitted and received over special lines provided by the telephone service but they are very slow. A message typed on the Hotsun telex is addressed to another telex subscriber where it is printed on his telex machine. Similarly incoming messages are printed on the Hotsun telex machine where the operator can receive them and then relay the message to the appropriate department. Originally this was done by sending the office boy around with the printed output but now the information can often be passed on by using the computer system.

Advanced electronic office software has now made it possible for all the Hotsun word processor operators to prepare and send telex messages, thanks to a clever link between the computer and telex system. By this means, messages can be sent to outside companies. The telex operator is still employed and the telex machine is still used to send messages, but the telex operator has a new gadget to play with.

Len took you back to the main reception area and showed you the **facsimile transmission** machine, usually referred to as **FAX**. The receptionist who was operating it explained what it did.

Essentially, it looked like a duplicating machine. A document could be placed on the bed of the machine and scanned. Instead of producing a photocopy, it divided the document into sequences of numbers which were then transmitted over the telex system. At the receiving end a similar machine reassembled the numbers into a document and then printed it out. Len explained that the major advantage of this over electronic mail was that it did not matter what the document contained. Whether it was handwritten or included drawings, the machine sent all the dots and squiggles just as they appeared on the original document. It was vitally important in Hotsun when documents requiring a signature had to be sent to Japan or Amsterdam in a hurry. The technical departments in the company tended to use FAX for sending technical drawings from one installation to another.

On glancing at a clock on the wall, you suddenly realised how late it was getting and how much time you had spent at Hotsun. It was time to prepare for the evening's festivities; so you handed in your badge and entered the time of departure in the visitors' book. Len then drove you back to your hotel.

That evening you attended the reception, which fully lived up to your expectation. As much food and drink as you could consume at Hotsun's expense. The speeches were short and entertaining, the prizes were presented to the top dealers in the country, and you were introduced to such celebrities as Malcolm Honeysett, the rally driver, tipped to win Hotsun the next world championship. In general, a good time was had by all.

Assignment 10

1   When you return to Westpool Motors John asks you for a complete report on what was said and what happened. In giving him the information you mentioned the pilot scheme for ordering spare parts which Len had described to you. John was extremely interested and felt that, if possible, Westpool Motors should try to get involved as soon as possible, though he did want some time to discuss the full implications of such a system. So he asked you to produce a list of benefits and disadvantages (if any) of the scheme.

Write out this detailed list of the benefits and drawbacks of the proposed system of giving each regional dealer a terminal so that spare parts orders can be keyed directly into the Hotsun computer. Your list should include benefits to both Hotsun and to Westpool Motors.

2   On your return you started to think about other ways in which the computer could be used at Westpool Motors. One possibility for the future was to transfer personnel details to the computer system. At present the company maintains a card index of all personnel in its employ. Employees' names, addresses, telephone numbers are recorded, along with details such as payroll numbers, job titles and job qualifications. It so happens that Hotsun run training courses for mechanics, to give them specific training on certain aspects of the range of Hotsun cars. One such course is on fuel injection systems, another on automatic transmission, and there are general courses on how to repair and maintain Hotsun cars. It is important that the personnel records contain details of the courses that the mechanics have attended, so that future training requirements can be scheduled.

You have decided to do a full systems analysis on the current personnel system. This requires the following:

a) A feasibility study giving details of the present system and an outline of how this system may be improved. If it is thought suitable to transfer the card index file to a computer you may well look at file management systems available for your computer system rather than contemplate writing programs to carry out the tasks required. The feasibility report should indicate how the system is to be used, costs involved, and benefits to be gained.

b) A system design giving details of any computer programs required (outline design only). Designs and layout for the required file structures should be given. This means that the record layout should be shown to indicate the fields required, the sizes of those fields and the type of file access required. Any forms or documents that may be required should be designed at this stage and copies should be included.

Remember: The system should provide for (i) setting up the files in the first place, (ii) adding records to the file as new members of staff join, (iii) deleting records as members of staff leave, and (iv) interrogating the files to find specific pieces of information quickly.

3 Len produces a progress report on his current project for Mr Yamamoto at the Japanese headquarters. List the stages involved in producing this report from the original handwritten draft to its final reception by Mr Yamamoto, if he uses a conventional typing pool and the normal postal system for delivery. Give some indication of the time involved, and compare this with the possible time saving by using electronic mail.

Exercise 6

1 Outline the respective roles of a systems analyst and a computer programmer in the design and implementation of a new computerised system.

2 Shortly before the motor vehicle licence of each car is due for renewal, the Department of the Environment sends a reminder to the owner of the vehicle. A computer is used to prepare the reminder by printing the information on a standard form.

On one section of the reminder are printed particulars regarding ownership and particulars of the vehicle concerned. If these particulars are correct the owner is invited to tear off this section and return it together with the tax due. If the particulars are not correct (e.g. the car has been resprayed a different colour) the owner is required to apply for a new licence on a separate form on which the changes can be recorded. New licences are subsequently despatched by post.

Outline, with the aid of a systems flowchart, how the computer can be used, in conjunction with the above procedure, to issue licences and to correct the computer's information regarding each vehicle. You should assume that the computers records are held on magnetic tape.

(Cambridge)

Glossary

bulletin board   File on a computer system which is used to store messages that can be accessed by other users of the system.

coding sheet   Form on which programmers write the lines of instructions which make up a program.

document keyword index   An index which covers all the documents on a word processing system. By looking up a word in this file the names of all the documents containing a reference to the word can be produced.

electronic mail   System which uses a computer to store messages which can be addressed to, and received by, other users.

electronic mailbox   File on a computer system which is used to store messages sent to a particular user by other users of the system.

facsimile transmission   System which allows the transmission of diagrams, photographs or documents over the telex system.

FAX   Abbreviation used for facsimile transmission system.

live running   Using a computer system to perform the task it is intended for rather than testing it alongside another system (see *going live*).

modem   A device to connect a computer to the telephone system, so enabling it to communicate with terminals or other computers. (*MOD*ulator *DEM*odulator unit).

multiplexor   Mechanism which allows several devices to share a single communications line.

terms of reference   Guidelines laid down to govern the areas that a study is supposed to cover.

test files   Set of files containing test data designed to find bugs in a program or limitations in the use of a system. These may have to be specially written for the testing stage of a project.

8 Hotel booking and administration –
Holiday Hotels

8.1 Holiday Hotels' organisation

The morning after the reception you were sitting in the hotel restaurant having breakfast when a very businesslike gentleman joined you at your table. He introduced himself as Bart Card, the hotel manager, and asked if everything was to your satisfaction. You asked whether he gave the same personal service to all of his customers. He said that he would like to be able to, but generally it was not possible. However, Hotsun motors were such good clients that he liked, whenever possible, to provide a little extra service. Whenever foreign visitors came to the Hotsun headquarters they were booked in to this hotel, and of course the guests attending the celebrations were all staying there and had used the conference centre for the previous evening's reception. The hotel was used mainly by people with business in London or for conferences, so they were used to large numbers of foreign guests and business people. It was conveniently situated with very good rail and road links with London and the Midlands, and was sufficiently distant from the capital to be quiet.

After a while Bart asked how you had been passing the time during your stay. When you described your visit to the Hotsun installation, he detected your interest in computers. He said that he had never expected to be involved with them at all when he first started in the hotel trade, but now information processing was everywhere. The small family hotel or guest house may survive by just doing the accounts and confirming the odd booking, but when you work for a large chain of hotels like this one the information flow is world wide.

During the discussion that followed you realised that looking after a hotel the size of the Holiday Hotel was the equivalent of running a village. There were of course the obvious staff—receptionists, waiters and bar staff, who served the guests directly, but behind the scenes there were also laundry staff, chambermaids, cleaners and maintenance staff making sure that the place was clean, tidy and comfortable. The restaurants and bars were supported by the cooks and kitchen staff. This meant that a small army of people had to be employed to make the hotel work. Once you had people working for you, it became necessary to look after them, and so a personnel department was needed. Large amounts of money were required to pay for goods and materials; this and the considerable revenue from guests, bars and restaurants and made it necessary to have an accounts department too. So you now began to appreciate a little of what Bart's job involved. He had to ensure that everything ran smoothly and that guests came to the hotel. While each section and department had its own manager or supervisor it was important for him to be kept informed about the running of each section.

Generally he said that he really enjoyed his job, but the meetings he had to attend and the reports he had to read to help him to keep informed meant that little time was left for him to meet guests. The problems were increased by the fact that this particular hotel was one of 1750 owned by an American company. The whole chain dealt with 80 million roomnight bookings each year, each one being part of an information processing operation. The bookings were combinations of individuals staying overnight or parties of people for several nights. The types of room available varied from single accommodation to the suites of rooms favoured by the rich. A computer system was installed in 1982 to help to organise these bookings and it certainly had eased the workload.

Breakfast was just finishing and you had decided to go and do some sightseeing. Bart suggested that before you left he would give you a quick look behind the scenes at how a large hotel chain worked.

It was considerably later in the day when you finally met Bart again and took up his offer. In his office he gave you some of the background to the company. American in origin, it believed in providing the best service and accommodation available. The company spread throughout the world during the 1960s and 70s and now had at least one hotel in nearly every major city in the world. Obviously the facilities available varied but they all offered some degree of luxury. Some had saunas, swimming pools or private cinemas and most had convention halls or conference centres. In fact these centres were a major source of income. Many companies, like Hotsun, arranged a convention or exhibition and then booked accommodation for those attending as a package deal.

The customers, in general, fell into a number of categories. Tourists stayed at the hotel because it was in pleasant surroundings and convenient for London. Included in this group were the couples on honeymoon who were booked into the honeymoon suite and got flowers sent to the room by the management. These extra little services helped to make the occasion a little special. As far as the resources of the hotel were concerned, honeymoon couples tended to be the least demanding.

Other tourists might arrive as single parties, taking advantage of special weekend break holidays provided by the hotel or they might be part of a large group booked by a tour operator or agent. A lot of American tourists arrived this way, spending a few days in England as part of a tour of the major cities of Europe. Of course you had already discussed the main client of the hotel, the businessman, who either had business in the hotel or was taking advantage of the good transport links with other areas.

8.2 Booking system

Bart said that everybody's stay at the hotel always started with a booking. The initial enquiry could be made in a number of ways, by telephone, telex, letter or Prestel and it could come from literally anywhere in the world. The booking system had to use the full range of communications systems available to cope with this situation. The proud boast of this hotel chain was that a booking could be made at a Holiday Hotel anywhere in the world by contacting the reservation centre, and the whole process only took three minutes. He noticed your look of disbelief, so he directed you out of his office and down into the administration area of the hotel.

In a large office a number of ladies were sitting at VDU screens. Each was wearing a headset with earphone and a microphone connected to the telephone system. It looked more like an air traffic control centre than a hotel. You were taken to one of the terminals where a call had been received from a secretary trying to book rooms in Paris for a group of businessmen. The VDU operator, Pat Key, was just starting to process the enquiry when you arrived. She had typed in the destination 'PARIS' in response to the initial prompt on the screen. After a short pause the names of two hotels in the Paris area appeared on the screen. She selected one of them and typed in its reference number. The screen flashed a request for the date of the required booking and Pat asked the caller for the information. As the date was relayed to her she typed it on to the machine and the screen displayed the STATUS page for the Mirabeau Hotel for the given date. From this screen she could find information about the hotel itself; number of rooms; free sauna; swimming pool; 20 km from the airport and also a list detailing the type, charge and number of rooms available on the requested day. At the bottom of the screen was a line which said

ENTER BOOKING DETAIL (Y/N)

Pat held a conversation with the girl at the other end of the line as they discussed the relative merits of the rooms, the charges and whether hire cars would be available as well as other details which Pat could give from the information on the screen. After a short time she pressed the 'Y' key to enter the booking. The screen changed and Pat entered the names of the people for whom the booking was being made and the type of accommodation required. At the end of this process the screen displayed

BOOKING CONFIRMED – Number 80A9835E
WRITTEN CONFIRMATION REQUIRED (Y/N)

Pat told the caller that the booking had been made and read out her booking confirmation number. She then read through the details (Fig. 8.1) from

```
CONF NUMBER 80A9835E
HARRISON/MR/D    PARTY OF 1
PARIS, FRANCE - MIRABEAU          PHONE-23/723-1277
274 RUE ST. JEAN
PARIS
HAS RESERVED    1 BASIC STANDARD
THU FEB 28    1 NIGHT
HELD FOR ARRIVAL BY 6PM



          MR HARRISON
          AMALGAMATED METALS LTD.
          CHICHESTER
          CH1 5RX


- - - - - - - - - - - - - - - - - - - - - - - - - - - - - -

UKL 74 00/85/00
TAX 15 PERCENT    XP LB 5         ZE
RB LB 5
02/18/86
```

Why make two phone calls when you can make one?
The HOLIDEX Computer is linked to the
International reservations network of
Hertz. So, when you book your next
Holiday Hotel, you can book your Hertz
car at the same time.
Most important of all TRAVEL AGENT'S
COMMISSION IS FULLY PROTECTED.
Call us on 01–722 7755 and we will tell you more.

Fig. 8.1 Holiday Hotels' booking confirmation

the screen giving the date, destination, names of the people and type of accommodation booked to ensure that the customer had all the details. Finally she asked if written confirmation was required. Obviously the answer had been 'yes' because she entered this on her keyboard and then thanked the caller for her enquiry.

In the corner of the room a printer started to produce a **hard copy** of the details on a booking confirmation form which could be sent to the customer and Pat's screen returned to the booking enquiry menu display. The enquiry had been made and booking confirmed and the whole thing had taken no more than a couple of minutes.

```
Holiday Hotels Booking
System Rev 3.2




                      BOOKING  ENQUIRY  MENU


                   1.   BOOKING ENQUIRY

                   2.   DELETE BOOKING

                   3.   CHANGE BOOKING DETAILS

                   4.   ADMINISTRATIVE SYSTEM

                   5.   EXIT




Please enter number of required choice (1 - 5) -
```

Pat took advantage of the break between calls to explain that the computer set up a record for each booking made. This contained details of the name, address, destination, booking confirmation number, date and various other data. These details could be called up from any terminal on the network if necessary so that reservation details could be checked. It was not even necessary to remember the reservation confirmation number since the programs handling the information included sophisticated search techniques which enabled booking details to be found even if only part of the data was known. Pat even remembered a case recently when it was necessary to trace a booking made for a Mr Spence, Spense or Spenser in either Zurich or Geneva. After typing the enquiry in at the terminal it took only a few seconds to find that a booking had been made for a Mr Spense at a hotel in Zurich. Fortunately this sort of problem did not arise very often.

A call came through for Pat and she was back at work. This caller had booked a room for three days at a hotel in Frankfurt but his plans had now changed and he had to spend the first two of those days in Amsterdam. Would it be possible to change the Frankfurt booking for one in Amsterdam instead? Pat said that there was no problem and she keyed in the booking confirmation number to call up the original booking details.

While the details of the new booking were being entered you noticed that from time to time the numbers showing the number of rooms available changed. Bart explained that the changes indicated rooms being booked (or cancellations) entered from other centres. The system worked in what was called **REAL TIME**. As the bookings were made, the files had to be updated immediately and the information displayed on the terminals to avoid the possibility of double booking a room. Otherwise, if the Amsterdam hotel only had one room left and Pat was processing this customer's enquiry at the same time as an operator in Chicago, and if the system was not operating in real time, it would be possible for both customers to book the room. The manager of the hotel in Amsterdam would have to sort out the resulting fight to decide who had the right to stay in the room.

This system puts great demands on the computer equipment which has to be able to deal with 900 000 enquiries each day. When you looked round the room you could believe that, as all the girls were busy dealing with calls from all parts of the world.

As you walked through the reception area after leaving the booking centre Bart gave you some technical details. To add to the problems he added that the computer that they were using was actually situated in America and required telephone and satellite links to handle the communications. The original system had cost $13 million and in the USA alone information was passed from 2300 computer terminals. This was international information processing on the grand scale, with 27 million roomnight bookings being handled.

You were impressed by the figures and wondered how they could justify such expenditure. Bart said that because of the improved information flow, the speed with which bookings could be made, confirmed or changed, organisations were willing to use this hotel chain rather than others which were not able to respond so fast. This meant that the number of bookings was increasing purely because of the system. Of course another side of this was that the management in the USA could use the computer to obtain information on which it could base policy decisions. Hotels that were extensively used could have facilities improved or the company could decide where to build new hotels by using the overall roomnight bookings as one of the pieces of information on which to base its decision.

As you passed the main reception desk you noticed a VDU screen and casually mentioned this to Bart. He said that it was used to call up the reservation details when a guest signed in. This meant that any special requirements which had been requested, such as connecting doors between rooms, could be checked and confirmed as the guest registered.

Assignment 11

1 Some time after your trip round the Holiday Hotel booking centre you started to think of all the times when you have to make reservations. Most of these situations might use a computer system similar to that at the hotel.

Make a list of all of the situations when you have to book a seat or make a reservation of some kind.

2   Take one of the situations which requires a booking to be made and write a brief description of how the reservations are handled at present.

3   Your local sports hall where you play squash and badminton has just installed a small computer to handle court bookings. It is also used to deal with the five-a-side football bookings. During your conversation with Bart Card you mention this and he seems extremely interested.

Give a brief description of a small system which could be used for this purpose. Describe the hardware that would be required and the details of the data which would have to be processed. (You may find a visit to your local sports hall beneficial.)

4   You may have access to a demonstration booking system in your school or college (airline and theatre systems are available). Use this to make a reservation and check on seat availability. (You will have to get hold of the relevant documentation which will explain how to do this.)

8.3   Hotel administration

Bart led you to another large office where a number of people were working. As you walked along, he said that the administration of the hotel required more than just the booking system. Restaurants and bars had to be kept stocked and services had to be maintained. A team of engineers were kept busy with repair jobs – unblocking washbasins, repairing broken showers and keeping all the fixtures and fittings in order. This sort of work entailed processing an enormous amount of data, and the production of paperwork, such as letters to outside contractors for major work, orders to suppliers, and so on. Work to be done had to be listed, and job sheets for completed work had to be checked.

The usual material for the day-to-day running of the hotel, such as soap and bed linen must be ordered and paid for. It was a little bit like doing the family housekeeping for a family of 2000.

Most of the people in the office were using word processors to produce letters or fill in forms but you were taken past them to the desk of Mike Dodgson, the financial director, who was sitting in front of a microcomputer. The screen was full of columns of figures, and Mike was deep in thought when you arrived. Bart asked if it was time to start looking for a new job. Mike laughed and said that he had been looking at the figures so that he could prepare a financial report for the directors. Actually they were not too bad and Bart's future, for the next six months at least, was secure. Mike said that he had been doing some forecasting from a **spreadsheet** program. He explained that the finances were very complex and that certain elements tended to be interdependent. The bar takings were depended on the number of guests. The number of guests depended on the number of bookings for conventions and exhibitions, and these in turn might depend on foreign exchange rates or the cost of travel if foreign visitors were involved. Since this hotel relied to a large extent on visitors from abroad, this type of information was important.

To make financial forecasts you record all the financial details for a certain period and then use them to try to predict what is likely to happen in the next period. The further ahead you try to predict, the less accurate you are likely to be. All sorts of unknown factors may present themselves, so to attempt to overcome these you introduce some WHAT IF? factors. For example, you can look at the cost of energy for the hotel for the last year and work out what it is likely to be for the coming year, but WHAT IF the gas boards put up the cost by 10 per cent and at the same time we get a sudden cold spell which requires the heating to be put on for an extra month?

Mike typed a few instructions on the keyboard and the figures disappeared to be replaced by another set. The problem we have just talked about is a very real one for which in the 'olden days' – well, a few years ago – all the figures would have been worked out with pencil and paper. Nowadays with the arrival of financial forecasting it is not sufficient to produce a single answer. Really you must try to work out what happens when all the factors are in your favour and get a 'best situation' and then work out the 'worst situation' and hope that real events produce a result somewhere between the two. This means that a lot of calculations have to be carried out. Now we use **electronic spreadsheet** programs on computers to do the hard work. He pointed to the screen. Here we have the energy figures for the last year. On the screen was a matrix of numbers with each column representing a month and each row representing elements of the energy consumption. One row gave details of the number of units of electricity used by the hotel in each month, one for units of gas and so on. Along the bottom was a row giving details of the total cost of energy for each month.

Mike said that we could look at the problem we had outlined earlier. He moved the cursor on the screen to the charge for gas and typed in a figure 10 per cent greater than the one already there. The screen rippled as this figure was transferred to each of the other columns and the totals were recalculated. Now what if the number of units of gas and electricity used in April are increased by, say 5 per cent to take into account the cold spell? Once again the screen rippled and new totals were produced. Mike said that it had taken just a few minutes to answer those questions but many calculations had been carried out. This particular spreadsheet was one of many stored on discs dealing with the hotel finances. By looking at these sets of figures and playing around with them it was possible to make some reasonable guesses at what was likely to happen in the future. Supposing the energy forecast turned out to be true, then it might be necessary to put up the prices to cover the extra cost – but by how much? Again these spreadsheets could help the manager to come to a reasonable decision based on predictions of how many guests are likely to stay and the number of conferences and so on.

You asked what happened if Mike got it wrong. He explained that the computer was only a tool to help in this decision making. The results obtained were only as good as the data supplied and the questions asked. By using the computer it was possible to do the calculating faster and get answers to more questions, but ultimately it still required the skill, knowledge and business sense of a good management team to make a success of the business. If Mike got it wrong, Bart would have to make decisions based on poor information. When he got it right the decisions would be based on good information and obviously they should be good decisions. In either case the result should be better than decisions made on no information at all, which was often the case before the computer was available.

You thanked Mike and Bart for the time that they had spent showing you around and explaining that there was more to running a large hotel than meets the eye. It was now time for you to pack and return home. Tomorrow you would have to go to work and report on the proceedings to John Jackson.

Assignment 12

1 You decide that a spreadsheet would be a useful way to keep check of your own expenses and financial forecasting. Use a spreadsheet package (VU-CALC, BEEBCALC, SUPERCALC, etc.) to set up the following worksheet. (You may have to refer to the relevant documentation to allow you to do this.)

	Week 1	Week 2	Week 3	Week 4	Week 5	Week 6	Total
Income							
Expenses							
Travel							
Food							
Drink							
Clothes							
Sundries							
Total							
Balance							

Put in all the headings (you may want to change some to suit your own spending pattern).

Fill in the actual amounts spent over the last six weeks. Use formulae to calculate the total expenditure (the sum of the expenditure ROWS) and the total spent on each item (the total of the expenditure COLUMNS)

Use formulae to calculate the BALANCE ROW (INCOME – EXPENDITURE)

Where possible copy formulae along rows or columns – make the program work for you.

You should now be able to see your personal expenses sheet at a glance. Save this worksheet.

2 Use the worksheet from Question 1 and add a column at the end with the heading 'Average'. Work out the average spending on each item in the sheet by dividing the Total column by six.

3 Use the worksheet to see what would be the effect of a 6 per cent rise in your income at the same time as an approximate rise in your travelling expenses of 2p per journey.

4 One of the things that interested you when you were looking around the Holiday Hotel was the subject of billing. You asked Bart Card whether the booking system produced the bills and he replied that at present bills were prepared manually but that a microcomputer was being installed to make them up in the near future.

Such a system would have to record the client's name, room number and an account reference number (perhaps the booking number). The bill details would then consist of combinations of bills from bars, restaurants and room service, in addition to the fee for the room(s).

Work out an outline design for a system that could deal with this problem and provide the final bill for the customer and a copy for the hotel.

Your design should include:

a) brief details of the type of equipment required (this need not be too technical);

b) a description of what each record on the files should contain;

c) a description of how the bill details will be collected and entered into your system.

d) details of any checks carried out to ensure that the details are correct.

Your system does not have to be computerised if you think a manual system will suffice.

A diagram or systems flowchart may help you to describe the system you would like to use.

A visit to a hotel to talk with the staff may help you to formulate a system to deal with this situation.

Exercise 7

1 A group of hotels share a computer on which it runs a room reservation system. The system uses three files. The first file gives the number of rooms of each type available in each hotel for each day up to one year ahead.

The second file lists details of advanced bookings. For each guest it has the name and address, the date of arrival, the length of stay, the type of accommodation and the amount of the deposit.

The third file is a ledger which has a record for each resident in the hotels. Every time a guest incurs a charge it is added to his record.

a) What on-line equipment would be installed at each hotel?

b) What kind of backing store would be most useful in this application?

c) Which files would need to be updated and how would they be altered when an hotel receptionist receives a telephoned enquiry for a room reservation?

d) Which files would need to be updated and how would they be altered when a person who has reserved a room arrives at the hotel?

e) Which files would need to be updated and how would they be altered when a guest is ready to leave the hotel?

(WMEB)

2 Computers and computerised equipment are increasingly being introduced into business management and office work.

a) Describe the changes which have occurred, or are likely to occur, because of the introduction of computer based technology.

b) State the advantages to management, other workers and the public brought about by the introduction of such technology.

c) Describe the changing pattern of employment, both in terms of numbers employed and the type of work carried out as a result of such technology.

(JMB)

Glossary

booking confirmation number   Unique number assigned to each booking to identify it. It becomes a key field on the booking records file.

booking system   Method of reserving seats on aeroplanes or in theatres or rooms in hotels and recording the reservation. Details may be recorded manually, or recorded and held on a file accessible by computer.

electronic spreadsheet   Computer program which allows values and calculations to be entered in rows and columns. Change a value and the results are automatically recalculated (see **spreadsheet**).

financial forecasting   The art (science?) of trying to work out the financial requirements/profits of an organisation.

financial report   Document containing the details of the income/expenditure of an organisation and probably a financial forecast as well.

hard copy   Report printed on paper.

menu display   Display, usually on a VDU screen, which gives details of a number of options that the program can perform. The user may then choose the option required.

REAL TIME   Method of using a computer in situations where time is a major consideration. The computer performs the tasks required of it *immediately* rather than at its convenience.

search   Process of finding a particular record on a file. The required record must be identified by a SEARCH KEY which is one of the fields on the records. Search is one of the main uses of computer systems because of the speed with which they can read and compare data.

spreadsheet   A sheet of paper 'spread' out on floor or desk, such that financial details can be entered on it in rows and columns. Calculations performed on these figures can be used for financial forecasts.

update   The process of changing the details on a file to reflect the current state of affairs. This will usually involve combinations of adding new records, deleting old records and changing the information on records on the file. May refer to manual or electronic file processing.

9 Banking systems –
Barwest Bank

Shortly after your return from Hotsun you were out shopping when quite by chance you met Penny Banks, a girl you had not seen since you left school. She was as pleased to see you as you were to see her, so you suggested that you should meet later in the week, have a meal together and chat over old times.

The following Thursday after work you went to the White Swan to meet Penny. She was already there, sitting in a quiet corner drinking orange juice. You got yourself a drink and joined her. For a time you chatted about people you had been at school with and what they were doing now. Fred Jones, who made a mess of everything he had done at school was now a management trainee with an oil company. Jane Smith had joined a rock group and gone to Germany. Eventually you started talking about what had happened to both of you since school. Penny was now working for Barwest Bank in the High Street and was enjoying it very much. You told her about your job and the recent trip to Hotsun, and put just the right emphasis on the service and hospitality to make her a touch envious.

Penny noted your interest in computers (it really would have been difficult to miss it) and said that banking was all about computers and information processing. You expressed surprise, saying that you thought that it was about money. She said that really very little real money was used. Instead, banks and building societies for that matter, concentrate their efforts on processing information about money. Somebody must actually transfer all the millions of pounds concerned from account to account but as far as she could see most of the transfers were carried out by computer.

9.1 Cheques

Penny took the acts of writing and cashing cheques as an example. So many transactions were carried out by this means that the banking system would collapse without computers, yet no cash actually needed to change hands. At the end of a transaction one computer deducts the amount of a cheque from the total on record as being deposited in one account and another computer adds the same amount to that recorded as being deposited in another account.

You were now very interested. Cashing cheques had been something you had done frequently without really understanding what happened, so you asked Penny to explain further.

She said that if she wrote a cheque and gave it to you in payment for goods received then you would take it and present it to your bank where you would complete a paying-in slip, which is a request to credit the

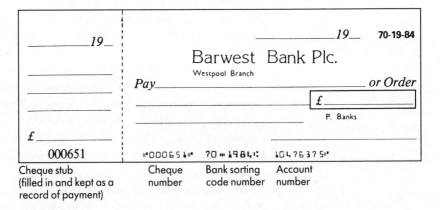

Fig. 9.1 A cheque

money to your account. The cashier would give you a receipt for the cheque and pass both it and the paying-in slip to a bank clerk. She added that in her branch of Barwest Bank the details of the cheque would also be keyed in to a computer terminal.

The cheque would be passed on to a remittance clerk who would stamp the cheque with the branch stamp. It is very unlikely that the **payee** and **payer** both have their accounts at the same branch or even with the same company, so all the cheques being cashed have to be sorted according to the bank at which the account is held. If your account is with the Midcounties Bank, this cheque would have been presented at one of their branches, but the money is to be paid from an account at the Barwest Bank. They will have to sort out all of the cheques to be drawn on Barwest accounts and put them together. The same will happen for cheques drawn on all other banks.

The next stage is for all the cheques to have their values printed on them in magnetic ink characters similar to those along the bottom of the cheque itself, so that details can be read directly from the cheque and input to a computer. A clerk operates a special typewriter which adds the magnetic ink characters and at the same time totals the amounts of money on the cheques of the different banks and lists all the cheques that pass through. Later in the day the cheques and lists are sent to the Midcounties Bank Clearing Department in London.

The next morning all the cheques presented at Midcounties branches throughout the country are dealt with by the clearing department. First they are put into boxes according to the bank to which they belong. Your cheque would go into the Barwest box. The cheques are then exchanged with the other banks for any Midcounties cheques they have received. This is done at the Bankers' Clearing House in Lombard Street, London. Your cheque is now returned to the clearing department of the Barwest Bank where all other similar cheques are sorted into packages for each of the branches. This is done by a machine linked to a computer. The magnetic ink on the bottom of the cheque is read and gives details of the branch, the account number and the cheque number. From this the computer can control a machine which directs the cheques into a series of collecting hoppers. The cheques are fed in at one end and the sorted batches are removed from the hoppers at the other.

During the next stage the cheques are all returned to the branches where the payers' accounts are held. A clerk checks that the details on the cheque are correct, that there is sufficient money in the account, and stamps it as 'paid'. The bank's computers then adjust the amounts in the accounts so that it appears as if the money had been paid over the counter.

You followed through the explanation and then asked what happened if there was not sufficient money available in the account to pay the cheque. Penny said that in that case instead of stamping the cheque as 'paid' it was stamped 'refer to drawer' and returned to the clearing house. The computer files would then be adjusted to reflect the fact that the cheque had not been cashed and your branch would return the cheque to you.

Surely some money changed hands somewhere along the line you asked. Penny said that when the transactions were going on at the Bankers' Clearing House the different banks' accounts with the Bank of England were adjusted and amounts exchanged. In effect the banks worked out how much they owed each other as a result of all of this money changing hands and money was transferred from one bank vault to another to keep the records straight.

9.2   Regular payments – standing orders

Apart from writing cheques, money can be transferred from one account to another on a regular basis by using **standing orders** or **direct debit mandates**. This means that the customer arranges with his bank to make a regular payment to another account. The details are recorded on a request form and passed on to the bank. A record is then produced on the computer giving details of when the payment is to be made, the account number, the amount and details of the account to be paid. At the appointed time the computer generates all the details required to allow the transfer to take place and debits the payer's account with the appropriate amount. Again, all that is processed is information relating to the required transfer.

It was time to eat and for a time the conversation changed to the topic of food as you carried out the more important (to you at the time) information processing task of examining the menu and deciding what to order.

9.3 Statements

When you had ordered and moved into the restaurant you asked Penny what would happen if a mistake occurred. She said that while all the money transfers were being handled by the banks' computers it was important that everybody was kept informed of what was going on. The bank keeps audit trail information consisting of reports that contain details of all of the transactions that the computer carries out. In the event of an error, which, she was quick to add, was very rare, it would be possible to trace manually any transaction from these reports. In addition, receipts

Statement of Account

P. Banks   **Barwest Bank Plc.**

Westpool Branch

Account No. 42345664

Date	Description	Debits	Credits	Balance
	Balance fwd.			206.18
JUN 1	CREDIT		340.00	546.18
JUN 2	081977	28.00		518.18
JUN 8	081978	28.00		490.18
JUN 10	CHARGES	3.23		486.95
JUN 15	CREDIT		90.00	576.95
JUN 20	121222	33.84		543.11
JUN 25	NORTHERN B/S	10.00		533.11
JUN 30	121223	100.00		433.11

Fig. 9.2 A statement of account

are always issued whenever anything changes hands, and details of all deposits and withdrawals are meticulously noted in bank books and ledgers as well as being entered on the computer system. A lot of the work carried out by people in banks consists of checking through computer printouts to answer queries or check that transactions have been completed success-fully. At the same time as the bank requires this information so does the customer. If the bank is transferring the customer's cash then he/she should be kept informed of where it is going. Generally customers receive a **statement of account** giving details of transactions carried out on a given account. These can be printed automatically by the computer and the customer may request one at any time. You asked if that meant that you could get statements at regular intervals and Penny said that you should ask your bank to send one to you every month if that is what you want. You said that at present you did not have any standing orders and as you cashed cheques rarely you had not bothered to ask.

9.4 Automatic cash dispensers

As you enjoyed your meal you casually remarked that the volume of cheques must be decreasing now anyway because everybody was now getting money from the machine in the wall. Penny disagreed and said that **automatic cash dispensers** (Fig. 9.3) were very controversial at present.

Banks installed them to provide a 24-hour service for customers. As with many new ideas, once one bank had installed them everybody had

Fig. 9.3 Automatic cash dispenser

to follow suit, but they were very expensive. You said that they must be worth while or the banks wouldn't use them. Penny went on to add that some of the installation costs could be saved by not employing so many staff. The more automated the system became the fewer the people required to run it. Your argument was that people were still needed to fill the machines, service and install them and supply the identity cards required by the customers.

While accepting that this was true to a certain extent, Penny went on to add that each machine was really a terminal, on-line to the bank's computer system. When you inserted your identity card the machine read information stored in its magnetic stripe and sent this to the computer which checked it was a valid card. You typed in your **personal identification number (PIN)** and the computer decided whether to talk to you or not. Assuming that your card was valid and the PIN had been entered correctly you could then use the terminal to withdraw money, find out how much was in your account or, in some cases, put money into your account. One result of this is that customers go to the bank continually throughout the day and night. This means that fewer customers have to attend when the bank is open so fewer clerks are required to deal with them.

Because the production of cash dispenser cards is automated, it requires few people and the money loaded into the machine is stored in cassettes which can be quickly replaced. All this increased efficiency requires fewer people.

One problem that banks are having to face as a result of introducing these machines is actually caused by the improved communications and by the **electronic funds transfer** facilities offered by computerised data processing systems.

Telecommunications networks connecting computers around the world enable money (or the information about it) to be quickly passed around the world. When the banks in the United Kingdom are closed at night, those on the other side of the world are open and doing business. It is possible to transfer money from British organisations to foreign ones and gain interest. The thought of drawing your savings out of the bank and investing them in Hong Kong overnight did not strike you as being a way of making a lot of money. Penny agreed! For the individual sending money around the world did not make sense, but for banks and multinational companies with billions of pounds to invest the interest could amount to millions of pounds a year.

Being curious, you asked what this had to do with cash dispensers. Penny replied that if the money was sitting in a machine in a hole in the wall, it was not available to invest elsewhere. On a typical weekend, for example, hundreds of thousands of pounds were waiting for customers when they should have been earning interest.

You were coming to the end of the meal and Penny suggested that you should both return to her house for coffee. She added that her parents would be pleased to see you after such a long time.

Assignment 13

1 You had managed to save some money and you decided to invest it. Banks and building societies offer a number of services and a number of different types of accounts. Study the literature produced by these institutions and create a table with the following headings

Name of company	Type of company	Name of account	Type of account	Interest rate	Mimimum amount required	Minimum time allowed	Special features

Under 'Type of Company' you should say whether it is a bank or building society. The type of account may be 'current', 'savings' or some other name given by the company. The 'special features' column may contain details such as whether a cheque book is issued or whether there is free banking if certain conditions are met.

This table provides a useful comparison of some of the facilities offered by banks and building societies and enables you to decide on the best place to make your investment.

2 When you go to the bank for a new cheque book you may be asked if you want 'open' cheques or 'crossed' cheques. Find out what the difference is and write a short explanation.

3 Your bank has only recently introduced automatic cash dispensers. They allow you to use your card to find out how much money is in your account. Your card can be used for this purpose at any branch, not just at the one where your account is held. You can also draw money, up to a certain limit, from your account at any cash dispenser. However, you have noticed that if you use the machine at certain times of the day it is unable to tell you your balance. The device is obviously connected to the bank's central computer (otherwise you would only get details from a limited number of branches) but it does not have access to account details all of the time. Explain how *you* think they work (details of how the money is counted are not required).

You could check your answer by asking at your local bank.

Exercise 8

The Bank Clearing House uses a magnetic ink reader/sorter to read cheques.
  a) Explain what the three codes at the bottom of the cheque are.
  b) Explain the function of the MICR and say why it is necessary.

9.5 The cashless society

Some time after your meeting with Penny you started to think about what she had said, and particularly about her reference to money transfers as information processing exercises. Quite often customers at Westpool Motors bought things without any cash changing hands. Items bought for other garages 'on account' were paid for at the end of the month when the invoices were sent out. Payment was usually by cheque as it was with many individual customers. We are gradually moving towards a society which can do without cash altogether!

9.6 Credit cards

Another increasingly popular method of paying for goods is by credit card and Westpool Motors will accept most of the common cards. Basically this is another type of **plastic money**.

The credit card company issues its customers with a plastic card or **badge** with the name and account number embossed on it. Usually the information is also coded on a magnetic stripe on the reverse of the card as well. When the customer first receives the card he/she signs it (this is a way of providing a **specimen signature**) and is given a **credit limit** governing the amount that can be 'spent' using the card.

A customer wanting to buy goods from Westpool Motors has the option of using a credit card. This is presented in payment in the same way as cash. Westpool Motors then has to find the book of payment slips for the appropriate company and fill in the description of the items purchased and the price. The payment slips and card are then placed on a machine which, when the handle is pulled, transfers the account details from the card to the payment slips. The customer then signs the payment slips and is given the top copy as a receipt.

The second copy of the payment slip is sent with all the others to the credit card company and in return Westpool Motors receives payment. At the credit card company the payment slips are fed through an **optical character reader** (OCR) which recognises the shapes of the characters and transfers the details to the company's computer system. This then updates the customer's record with details of the purchase and outstanding balance. The cheques for Westpool Motors and all the other firms which accept cards as payment are produced by the computer system.

Each month the computer produces a statement for the customer giving details of the purchases made, payments received and outstanding balance. This is sent out to the customer who then has the option of either paying off the whole of the outstanding balance or of making a partial payment. The credit card company can then make money by charging interest on any outstanding debt there may be at the end of the month.

Two types of credit card company exist at present. Major banks offer credit card facilities (Fig. 9.4) which are often extended to customers of the smaller banks. The remaining credit card companies operate solely to provide this type of service.

Fig. 9.4 Bank cards

9.7 Touch tone telephones

During your next meeting with Penny you mentioned that you were thinking of getting a credit card and she said that her bank offered one, and added that it was one step further towards the cashless society. At present it is only worth using a credit card or writing a cheque for fairly large amounts, but in future it may be possible to make all purchases this way.

Shops may have terminals instead of tills. These could consist of modified push button telephones with a slot in the top to accept a credit card. A customer would offer the credit card in payment for goods and this would be pushed into the slot. The telephone would then automatically dial the credit card company's computer and read the account number from the magnetic stripe. The shopkeeper could then key in a code identifying his/her business and tap in the value of the transaction. The computer could then arrange for the information relating to the transaction to be generated so that the shopkeeper's account was credited and the customer's account debited by the appropriate amounts. At the end of the month the shopkeeper would receive payment and the customer would be sent a statement giving details of recent transactions.

After hearing all this, you said that it was unlikely to happen and sounded a little far-fetched. Penny said that you, of all people, should believe it since some garages had already gone part of the way by installing petrol pumps that were capable of accepting payment by credit card. A customer entering a filling station at any hour of the day or night could use one of these pumps by pushing the card into a reader. If the card was valid it would then allow petrol to be dispensed and record the details of the transaction. The filling station owner could then retrieve this information and send it to the credit card company to be paid in the normal way.

Penny emphasised the point by saying that if more vending machines were produced to accept payment in this way, it might be feasible to get rid of cash altogether.

Assignment 14

1 One of the major problems that you had considered, when talking about the 'cashless society' was that of theft and fraud. Discuss this with the rest of your group and then list as many steps as you can think of that banks and credit card companies can take to reduce or eliminate the fraudulent use of stolen cheque books and credit cards.

2 You have decided that you would like a credit card. Obtain an application form to apply for one and fill it in. Look carefully at the questions that you have answered. Do you think that they are all relevant? If the answer is 'no' explain which questions you think are irrelevant and why.

3 You are quite interested in the idea of the cashless society. Discuss with the rest of your group how far we have come towards getting rid of cash altogether. List the goods and services that can be obtained now without the need for cash. Are there any situations now where cash is actually required? If so, list them.

Exercise 9

1 a) Compare optical character recognition (OCR), optical mark recognition (OMR) and magnetic ink recognition (MICR) for the input in terms of

   (i) the need for skilled data preparation staff;
   (ii) the means of verification;
   (iii) reliability and environmental factors.

b) Briefly describe an application of each method of data input in such a way that makes clear why the particular method is suitable for the chosen application.

(London)

2 Compare the type of work done by a bank clerk in the 1920s with the type of work done in the 1980s.

How has the use of computers helped the work of the banks?

How have the banks' customers been affected by the changes?

(SREB)

Glosssary

automatic cash dispenser   A machine which will give money to authorised customers. The customer must insert a card into the machine as identification. Other services may be available such as the ability to get a printout of the balance of the account.

automatic bank teller   Another name for automatic cash dispenser.

badge   Name given to a plastic identity card used as cheque guarantee card, credit card or similar. Often has a magnetic strip on the reverse side which can contain coded information which may be read by a machine.

cheque   Written order to a bank to pay a named person or organisation. Usually written on a specially designed form but may be written on anything.

clearing house   Central agency which sorts cheques and returns them to the bank on which they are drawn.

credit card   A 'badge' or plastic card which identifies the bearer as a person having an account with a credit card company. This allows the credit card holder to buy goods and pay the credit card company at a later date.

credit limit   The amount of money that a company will allow a customer to owe before it receives payment or stops supplying goods.

direct debit   The authority that a bank account holder gives to another person or company to allow them to draw money from his/her account. Often used to allow an organisation to withdraw yearly subscriptions (say) from members accounts.

electronic funds transfer   The ability to move money from one bank account to another by giving instructions to a computer.

MICR   *Magnetic Ink Character Recognition* – used mainly for reading amounts, account numbers, etc., from cheques. Relies on the fact that the ink has a high iron content and when magnetised each character produces a unique magnetic pattern which can be decoded by a reading machine.

payee   Person who is paid money.

payer   Person who pays some money.

paying-in slip   Form completed by a person paying money into an account, giving details of the amount paid and the account into which it should go.

PIN   *P*ersonal *I*dentification *N*umber – a number typed into an automatic cash dispenser to identify the owner of the identity card. This is a 'password' which is never displayed, hence cannot be used by anybody finding or stealing an identity card.

printout   Any printed listing produced on paper by a computer system.

specimen signature   A signature that is retained by a bank, building society or other organisation and can be compared with a signature given as authorisation to withdraw money. A method of identifying an account holder.

standing order   Authorisation given to a bank to enable it to make regular payments on a customer's behalf and withdraw the money from the account concerned.

statement   Document giving details of issues and receipts in a bank or building society account.

touch tone telephone   Telephone with push buttons instead of a dial. Each number can be recognised by the different tone emitted as the buttons are pushed.

10 Travel agents –
Trans Europe Travel

Summer was approaching and you decided that it was time to start thinking about holidays; so you toured the travel agents collecting brochures.

Eventually you decided on a package tour to Spain and went along to the local branch of Trans Europe Travel to book it. While you were completing the booking details and the assistant was filling in the relevant forms you noticed a number of VDUs on the counter and asked if the company was using a computer to handle bookings.

10.1 Prestel

The assistant said that they were **Prestel terminals**. Instead of buying its own computer the company made use of the service offered by British Telecom. This allowed people access to a computer as **information providers** or **users** or both. The information providers buy **pages** from British Telecom and put on them information that they think the users will want. These pages are records or **frames** which can be called up over a telephone link and displayed on a terminal.

The travel industry makes quite a lot of use of Prestel because the tour operators put information relating to holiday bookings on to it and all the major airlines use it to record their schedules and fares. Other information providers make sure that travel agents can keep up to date with exchange rates, hotel bookings and various other information.

You remembered that while you were staying at the Holiday Hotel you had been told that rooms could be booked through Prestel and you mentioned this to the young lady in the travel agent's. She said that this was the beauty of Prestel, it allowed two-way communication and so could be used to book theatre tickets, airline reservations or hotel rooms. She offered to give you a demonstration.

She switched on the VDU, pressed a key, and a sequence of numbers appeared on the screen as the built-in **auto dial modem** made the connection to the computer through the telephone network. A message appeared on the screen inviting the user to type in the password. The assistant hit a few keys which resulted in a series of dashes printing on the screen and the system then displayed a message. Hitting another key produced the main menu on the screen.

One of the items on this menu was an alphabetical list of information providers; so you selected this and another menu, giving page numbers corresponding to groups of information provided.

You decided that you would like to know the time of the next train to London. Selecting the page number which would lead you to the 'Bri' page you were then faced with a number of options all starting with these letters. One of them was British Rail; so you selected that page. As you had been moving through these menus a number at the top of the screen changed. This was the frame or page number and as you went through successive menus it increased. With each menu the number of digits increased as you delved deeper into the database. It seemed very slow and cumbersome to you but the assistant said that it was not necessary to go through the menus. If you knew the page number that you required you could key it in directly and it would go straight to that frame and display it. When you worked with the system for a reasonable length of time you began to remember the pages that you needed.

You found the British Rail information that you wanted and began to look at some of the other pages. When you accessed some of them a number would appear in the top right-hand corner of the screen. It was explained that the information providers made a charge for those frames and the value displayed was this **frame charge**. This money was added to the quarterly bill and it was then passed on to the information providers to help to recover some of their costs. Many large concerns spent a lot of money keeping their Prestel information up to date, sometimes changing it every couple of hours. The only way that they could afford to do that was to 'sell' the information to the users through the use of this frame charge.

10.2 Prestel facilities

Prestel offers not only information and the booking service but also a number of other facilities.

One such service is called **teleshopping**. It is available from some retailers and allows customers to access catalogues on their pages. They can then choose to buy items and key in the details to **answer-back pages**. These store the information on the computer. The customers can arrange payment by typing in a **charge account number** or credit card number. The retailer can then get this information from Prestel and arrange for the goods to be delivered.

The assistant who was demonstrating the system to you was obviously informed about all of the facilities available. She told you of an information provider in the Midlands who runs a club for Prestel users. Not only can they **teleshop** at local supermarkets but they can also book seats on day trips run by the club. Another service offered is a **homework helpline** which provides help with children's homework problems keyed in to the Prestel system.

A natural extension of this system is electronic mail. You said that you had come across that before. Your guide said that as soon as she accessed the system it checked her mailbox to see if there were any messages for her. Similarly she could send messages to any other Prestel user.

After you had finished the demonstration the girl signed off by pressing a few keys. As she did so she said that using this system allowed her company access to a number of the facilities of a large computer relatively cheaply. In addition the company could get access to a large amount of information provided by other organisations. The travel industry and financial institutions in particular found this very useful. In some cases, banks and building societies were starting to use the system to allow their customers to access their own accounts and check their balances. It was even possible, if you had accounts with certain companies, to transfer money from one account to another. You said that you had been discussing this sort of thing with Penny, and that this seemed to be one further step towards the cashless society. It is likely that in the future more people will find a use for the Prestel system.

10.3 Teletext

You said that the pages of information displayed on Prestel looked similar to those you had seen demonstrated in the television shop using **teletext**. The assistant seemed to have a reasonable knowledge of this system and said that there were indeed many similarities. Teletext pages are made up on a computer in a similar fashion to Prestel, but they are transmitted on spare lines along with those which go to make up the television picture. Everybody gets teletext information along with their television pictures but only those people with teletext decoders can actually display the text in a readable form.

The pages are selected by using the handset which controls the remote channel changing. As the pages are transmitted in sequence the decoder waits for the required page and then displays it on the screen and holds it until another one is selected. This means that the information provided is free if you have a teletext television set.

You said that it must be preferable to get the free information from teletext rather than pay through Prestel. The assistant replied that the teletext system gave limited information which is supplied by the television companies. The BBC has a system called **CEEFAX**, the IBA has **ORACLE** and they decide what information is to be transmitted. These systems are only one way; that is, the customer receives the information that the television companies decide to put out and there is no answer-back facility.

You remembered that your old aunt has teletext and she uses it to keep track of her favourite soap opera. If she misses an episode she can call up a page which contains a brief description of what has happened.

She is also a little deaf, so she makes use of another facility that teletext offers. As the information is transmitted along with the normal pictures it is possible to display both at the same time. For some programmes the television companies transmit **subtitles** on teletext pages. This means that your deaf aunt can watch programmes without missing half the dialogue.

This system can be useful when screening foreign programmes, for subtitles can be prepared and transmitted on teletext, thus saving the cost of having them put on to the film. The assistant added that this was a major use of teletext, and obviously, since the system was run by the television companies, a large proportion of the information transmitted related to television. It included programme guides and follow-up information on programmes, although a large number of general interest pages were also available.

As you left Trans Europe Travel you said that you would be back next month to pay for the holiday and you thanked the assistant for the Prestel demonstration. She said that most of the paperwork would be completed by then and laughed. Despite all this modern technology, most of the information is still collected and transferred by filling in forms and sending them from one place to another.

Assignment 15

1 You were very impressed with Prestel and you mentioned it to John Jackson when you returned to work. He decided that it might be worth looking at and asked you to find out what it would cost.

Produce a report giving the costings for

a) renting a Prestel terminal (some television rental companies do this);

b) buying a modem to connect the Westpool Motors microcomputer to Prestel (Modems are often advertised in the computing press);

c) the charges for using Prestel and any extra costs which may be involved.

2 If you can get access to Prestel use it to solve a problem for John Jackson. He has to go to a business meeting in Frankfurt. This will entail a trip to London where he hopes to visit a friend and stay overnight in an hotel before flying to Germany the following day. In Frankfurt he

will stay overnight and fly back to London the following day, hopefully returning home the same day.

Produce an itinerary for him giving the following:

a) time of a train to London getting in before noon (preferably with dining car);

b) first class return fare (at full rate);

c) name and details of a hotel which is convenient for the airport and which costs less than £50 per night;

d) details of a flight to Frankfurt which will arrive before 2.00 p.m;

e) the air fare;

f) details of an hotel in Frankfurt which is close to the city centre;

g) the charge for the hotel (in pounds sterling);

h) details of the return flight the following day;

i) train times for his return home.

(*Assume your home town is the start/end point*)

3 A large number of pages of information televised on CEEFAX and ORACLE relate to television programmes. Produce a list of ten items (say) which are not directly related to television.

How could the information you have listed have been obtained elsewhere?

Give the advantages and disadvantages of using teletext to obtain this information.

Exercise 10

(i) List two departments of national government which make use of large data banks.

(ii) For each department named describe the main use of the data banks.

(iii) choose one of the departments and list the advantages of the computerisation of such data banks for

a) the department concerned

b) individuals in society.

(iv) What possible effects could arise from storage of inaccurate data in the example chosen?

(v) Explain one main difference between PRESTEL and CEEFAX (or ORACLE).

(vi) List three kinds of use for PRESTEL and CEEFAX.

(Scot)

Glossary

answer-back Facility on publicly available computer systems to be able to enter data of your own.

auto-dial modem A modem which has the facility to dial a specified number and make the connection with a computer automatically.

CEEFAX Teletext system operated by the BBC.

charge account system which enables a customer to buy goods from a supplier and be billed for them later rather than paying over the counter. Most large stores operate charge account schemes.

frame The amount of information that can be displayed on a VDU screen.

frame charge Charge made to the user of a teletext system for accessing a particular screen full of information.

information provider Person or organisation which puts information on to a teletext system.

ORACLE Teletext system operated by the IBA.

page Unit of information on a teletext system made up of one or more frames.

PRESTEL Public database and teletext system operated by British Telecom.

subtitle Text displayed over a television programme. Often used to print English dialogue on foreign television programmes.

teleshopping System available through Prestel that allows goods to be chosen and paid for using terminal connected to computer system.

teletext System which allows information to be selected from a database and displayed on a television or VDU screen.

user Anybody who gets information from a teletext or other computer system.

11 Future developments

Several weeks after you had booked your holiday you received an invitation to a party through the post. Most of your friends were going and you were looking forward to meeting them. It was to be held at the home of Louise Brown which is a large place set in its own grounds. Louise's father, William Brown, owns a large engineering company in the town and he was footing the bill for the party. You arrived at about nine thirty, and found plenty to eat and drink; a disco had been set up in the drawing room (it really was that sort of house) and large numbers of people were milling around and enjoying themselves.

As the night passed, you eventually found yourself discussing the future amidst a group of friends, several of whom you had not seen for some time. Carl was very despondent. He had been unemployed for some time and said that he could see little prospect of employment. It seemed to him that machines were taking over jobs and people weren't needed any more.

11.1 Personal computers

The group conceded that computers did seem to be everywhere, even when it was not apparent that they were being used. At the same time they all had to admit that they had computers of their own at home. It seemed that most people had them because of fashion, and they used them for entertainment, to play games of various types. Many of the group thought that the home computer boom was over and that fewer people would buy them in the future. June said that really it depended on how they were to be used and what facilities they would offer. If they could only be used for playing games, the interest would remain so long as new games could be produced, but surely the computer had more to offer than that!

She had read about people using home computers for storing recipes.

A simple program gave ideas for recipes, worked out the cost for a given number of people, and provided lists of ingredients. The same computer could be used with a different program to keep track of home finances and help the children to learn as well as providing entertainment. All this could be done now, but very few people seemed to realise it. Most could see little further than the games.

11.2 Databases

Jay came in and said that it was rather short-sighted to use the personal computer for things within the home. Surely one of its major benefits would be to access information outside the home. By connecting the computer to the telephone system you could have access to **public database** systems such as Prestel. A number of other databases might be set up in the future which would be available on subscription. In the same way as you might join a book club now to get books on certain topics so you might pay a subscription which would allow you to access a computer containing a database with information on specialist topics. All the world's knowledge, as contained in books and other published materials, would one day be on computer systems. These systems could then be **networked** and anybody with a home computer and telephone would be able to gain access to the information they required without having to leave the comfort of their own home.

Everybody laughed as Jay's imagination seemed to be getting the better of him, but when you thought about seriously it no longer seemed far-fetched.

11.3 Electronic letters

You came into the conversation at this point and added that if they were setting up a worldwide network of computers to hold this body of know-ledge, why not make it a two-way system? Already we have the opportunity to do this in Britain through Prestel so why not extend it so that not only can you get information but also provide answer back? You explained that one advantage of this would be an extension of the existing electronic mailing systems. Nobody had heard of electronic mail so you had to explain it to them. You ended up by saying that a number of systems for passing messages from computer to computer already existed.

June said that she had come across such systems in large companies that have their own computer system, but it was not feasible at home. You disagreed. Prestel already offered the mailbox facility at a reduced rate to home users, and British Telecom also offered an electronic mail system called **Telecom Gold**. While this was obviously aimed mainly at industrial and commercial users it was also available to anybody who was willing to pay for it. Carl said that he did not see any point in using computers to send messages when we already had a perfectly good postal system.

The advantage of electronic mail is that it is sent immediately and received shortly afterwards. It is also available to the recipient wherever he has access to a computer terminal and telephone. The business applications are obvious. A salesman, for example, with an area in the north of Scotland and head office in the south of England can record orders on a portable computer. Later he can use the hotel telephone to transmit the order to the head office computer and receive confirmation that the order can be met.

While he is moving from one hotel to another he can also use the portable computer to download his mail from the company's central computer over the telephone. Replies can be sent off and all without anybody having to know his exact location. One major problem with letters is that they are not sent to people but to addresses. If the people are not at the address they do not receive their mail. This can be avoided with electronic mailing systems.

Carl remained unconvinced and said that it would not catch on. You reminded him that the same was said of the telephone and that seemed to have 'caught on' quite nicely.

11.4 Fibre optics

June said that she thought that if everybody used electronic mail the telephone system might not be able to cope with the demand.

Jay replied that scientists were already working on that one. The existing copper cables which carry telephone messages certainly would not handle the increased traffic, but fibre optics could. A fine thread of glass can be produced which allows light to pass along it like electricity flowing along a cable. The light can then carry messages in the form of high-speed pulses. The messages travel at the speed of light and the fibres are so fine that many thousand times the number of messages can be transmitted along a bundle of these fibres than along a copper wire of the same thickness. Gradually the existing cables will be replaced by fibre optic ones and then there will be enough capacity to handle a large range of communications.

If every house were connected up to this fibre optic cable network (in a way similar to that which connects subscribers to existing telephone networks) then not only could messages be switched very easily but also **cable television** would be generally available. This could allow thirty to forty television channels to be used. Some of these could be used for local broadcasts, operating in the same way as local radio.

Connecting local television, telephones and computers could open the way to the abolition of schools. Children could be taught at home from programmes broadcast on the 'educational channel', and pupils could interact with each other and the teachers through the computer/telephone system.

Carl liked the idea of thirty television channels. As he was unemployed he had little to do all day and he felt that pressing the buttons to change from channel to channel could give him a new interest in life.

11.5 Electronic cottage industry

You said that if there were systems like this one many people might be joining Carl. It was not that they would be out of work, but that for a large number of them there would be no need to go out of the house to go to work. The computer system could be used to connect the house to the office and home would become an extension of work. This is already happening in some industries in America where many workers are remote from their offices in an **electronic cottage industry**. Obviously everybody cannot work in this way. You felt that John Jackson would not like it if you decided that you were going to work from home, but if you had been a computer programmer, for example, a large proportion of your work could be carried out at home, provided the necessary link with the company computer existed.

This change in working patterns is just beginning to happen, and you though that it was definitely a trend which would continue in the future although inevitably there would always be some people who would go out to work even if only for social contact.

Carl said that he wouldn't mind working at home. In fact he wouldn't mind where he worked if he could get a job.

11.6 Robotics

At this point Louise entered the room and picked up the end of the conversation. She said that her father had been putting robots into his factories and that he therefore had to employ fewer people. The robots could be used to put materials on to the machines and take the finished products off. A computer controls each robot and makes sure that it performs checks for quality control as it handles the machining. To make different products entails changing the programs to make the robots carry out the tasks in a different way. June said that she had heard of factories in Japan where they produce goods around the clock and they only employ a security guard. Jay said that this was an exaggeration. His boss had recently come back from a tour of Japan and had visited factories there. There is little doubt that the Japanese were very well organised and used automated machines where possible.

Apparently the manufacturing process starts at the design stage, where a computer is used to run a series of **CAD/CAM** programs. Designers sit at terminals and key information into a central computer instead of using a drawing board to produce designs. This means that a lot of time normally spent redrawing and correcting drawing is saved. The **computer aided design** system can also display three-dimensional images of the product being designed. This gives the designer a far better idea of how his ideas will turn out.

Once the design has been produced the product can be divided into components and the **computer aided manufacturing** programs can be used to work out how each piece should be machined. The computer can then produce a **paper tape** which can be loaded on to a **CNC (computer numerically controlled)** machine. A computer on the machines then reads its instructions from the paper tape and performs the required machining operations. It may be that the CNC machine is a lathe or milling machine and it needs the item requiring machining to be precisely placed before it can work successfully. In this case, a **robot arm** controlled by a computer may be required to pick up items, decide which way round they are, and place them accurately on the machine. At the end of the process the arm may remove the component and check it against a standard for quality control purposes. This type of situation works well on a number of production lines where computer-controlled machines can handle repetitive machining or assembly operations, but people are still required to keep the machines running and service them. As yet the development and design work requires people, and fully automated production lines are expensive to install.

Carl said that he wouldn't mind a job looking after a robot. He could treat it as a sort of pet and make sure it had all the necessities of life.

June said that surely what she had said earlier was possible. Jay said that no doubt in the future, as robots became more sophisticated, and more computer power became available it might be possible for factories to exist and require very few people to run them. Computers would handle design and manufacturing operations.

You said that computer control of complex operations was already common.

11.7 Domestic appliances

You asked Louise whether they had a microwave cooker, an automatic washing machine and a dishwasher. She replied that they had all three and was surprised that you needed to ask. You said that all of them may have computers in them to handle the information processing and control operations.

The microwave may be the type on which you key in a code to represent the item cooking and the weight. A computer calculates the cooking time, switches on the oven and switches it off after the appropriate time has elapsed. Similarly with the washing machine. Tell it which wash you want and it controls the filling, heating the water, pre-wash, wash, rinse and spin cycles according to its built-in programs. In the future the improvements in robot technology may result in the home robot which carries out certain tasks. Digging the garden, taking the dog for a walk and so on.

A central computer in the house could deal with looking after the house in general. Controlling the central heating and air-conditioning, and switching lights on and off when people enter or leave rooms could be tasks assigned to it. It may be that the central computer could be used to pass instructions to the robot, so that a central file could be maintained giving details of the jobs it has to do. The computer could then work out the program required to enable the robot to carry out these tasks.

Jay did not see what all of this had to do with automated factories and you said that it was just another example of how our lives are gradually being changed with the increase in automation. Carl was beginning to look even more depressed. It looked as though the machines had it made and that he would never get a job.

11.8 Leisure

Jay said that Carl had a point. There was no point in producing goods if everybody was out of work and nobody could afford to buy them. You agreed and said that a number of alternatives might be available. One might be a collapse of society as we know it because of an increase in the differences between the few in work who earn lots of money and have everything, and the majority, out of work, and with no prospects of ever getting a job.

Another possibility was a change in working patterns. The increase in the number of consumers requiring the latest piece of equipment and the increase in productivity arising from the building of semi-automated factories could allow people to earn the same money while working a shorter week. Those who earn this money want to spend it on leisure activities, and this creates a demand for leisure goods and services. This allows more people to be employed in providing these goods and services and the cycle starts all over again.

Carl asked you if you would work a shorter week so that he could share your job. He promised that in return he would spend his money on leisure activities to provide a job for somebody else. You said that while you would like to help it was not possible just yet but **job sharing** may be another possibility for the future. Instead of employing somebody to work all week, an employer may employ two people to work three days each. This was already being tried, quite successfully, in some areas.

11.9 Laser discs and holograms

One thing was fairly certain. The leisure activities of the future would be different from today's. The linking of high technology to games gives rise to a number of possibilities.

Laser discs which store huge quantities of data on a plastic-coated disc like an LP record enable computer generated text and graphics to be combined with video pictures. At present these are being used to produce improved space invaders type games, but in the future they will be used for more sophisticated entertainment. Linked with **holograms** (three-dimensional pictures in space generated by laser) they could enable us to experience great moments of history, first-hand, in your living room, or a 'live' rock concert with high quality sound and full sized holograms of your favourite band for you to mingle with. Carl said that this sounded great, but surely with all of this capacity to collect, store and process data there was a risk that society would become a very different thing.

11.10 Privacy and security

If the information were controlled by the wrong people surely we might end up in a police state. Everybody agreed that the amount of information available might be useful, if it were all to be put together, under certain circumstances and for certain people. Jay said that perhaps this was not necessarily a bad thing. If the police had access to the information, it would help to keep the crime rate down and even help to catch criminals. That would be of benefit to all of us and if we were innocent it should not really matter what information was held.

June was not convinced and said that she did not think that it was right that people should hold information about her and that this information could be collected from a number of different sources. You pointed out that the information had always been there. She said that this was not the problem. As far as she was concerned one of the major worries was that in the future communications between computers would increase and that could lead to all the information being gathered into one central place by people who had no right to access it. She would have no control over who had it or what they did with it. You said that this was a valid point, and obviously the government thought so as well because it had just introduced new laws governing the collection and use of data. Under the Data Protection Act any organisation collecting personal data and keeping it on a computer system has to register with the Data Protection Registrar who will make sure that the use of that data is strictly controlled. Anybody who feels that data about them is incorrect or that data is being misused can appeal to the Registrar who will look into the situation. Everybody present thought that this was probably a step in the right direction and that hopefully the future would not produce problems of this kind.

It was now getting very late and with ideas of automated factories and homes run by robots, and of life-sized space invaders descending in glorious technicolour to be zapped by your hologram laser, buzzing in your head you tendered your farewells and made your way home.

The following week you bumped into Carl. He couldn't stop to talk as he was on his way to work. It seems the day after the party Louise's father had offered him a job—helping to install the robot arms in his new factory.

Assignment 16

1 You obviously have your own ideas of what is likely to happen in the future. Already you have lived through major social changes, some of which have been brought about by new technology.

Predicting what is likely to happen in the future is a very difficult task. So often science fiction turns into science fact in a very short period of time.

Write a brief set of notes giving your view of how business and commerce might change over

    a) the next ten years

    b) the next twenty-five years

Take into account the changes we have already seen in office systems (word processing and electronic mailing systems), manufacturing industries (computer aided design systems and robotics), and data processing (computer networks, cheap powerful microcomputers, improved worldwide communications). Where possible give reasoned arguments to back up your predictions rather than just letting your imagination take over.

2 The first major data processing project that we know of was the Domesday Book. To celebrate its 900th birthday a modern equivalent, the Domesday Project, was announced in 1985. The idea is to use modern technology to produce a data base giving as clear a picture as possible of what life is like in Britain in the 1980s. When finished, the information should be available for people to access. The data is to use a combination of computer and laser disc technology to allow fast retrieval of both text and pictures.

Find out as much as you can about the Domesday Project from the computer press and the library.

Give details of the type of information that you think may usefully be incorporated into such a project. For example you may think that the information on the electoral roll may be of value and should be included.

How do you think that such a database may be of value in say ten years' time?

Exercise 11

1 'In recent years there have been more computer crimes'.
  i) Explain what is meant by 'computer crimes'?
  ii) Give two specific examples of computer fraud.
  iii) Give two reasons why computer fraud is difficult to detect.

2 'The increased use of computers in many other aspects of life has caused great concern'
  i) Give two other causes for concern apart from fraud.
  ii) Give one way in which each of these causes may be reduced.

(AEB)

3 Distinguish between privacy of information and security of information giving one example of how each may be achieved.

(AEB)

Glossary

cable television   Television received along copper or fibre optic cables instead of by transmission through the air.

CAD   *C*omputer *A*ided *D*esign. Using a computer to help to produce the drawings required at the design stage of a project.

CAM   *C*omputer *A*ided *M*anufacture. Using a computer to produce programs (sets of instructions) for machines to allow them to carry out a manufacturing process.

CNC   *C*omputer *N*umerically *C*ontrolled. The type of machine that can decode and follow a set of instructions which it can read from a keyboard or paper tape.

cottage industry   Work that can be carried out at home rather than requiring an office or major workshop facility.

database   Set of related files – usually stored on a computer.

electronic cottage industry   A computer-related job that can be carried out from home – perhaps relying on telecommunications equipment to keep in touch with an office or other place of work.

fibre optics   Very fine glass threads which allow light to flow along them like electricity along a wire.

hologram   A three-dimensional image produced by a combination of laser technology and polarised light.

job sharing   System whereby two or more people are employed to do one job but instead of one person putting in a full working week each person works for a portion of the week only.

laser   Device which emits a very powerful pure light.

laser disc   A method of storing very large amounts of data as patterns of fine dimples on the surface of a disc. It is read by decoding the patterns produced by a laser light reflected off the disc surface.

network   A system of two or more computers capable of communicating with each other and passing data and programs to each other.

personal computer   Any small computer containing input, output, backing store and processor as a single unit capable of being used on a desk top.

portable computer   Small computer system capable of being carried around. Some have built-in power supplies but most require mains electricity supply to power them. Most will allow the keyboards to fold in and have a flat screen so that they pack into a briefcase sized package.

public database   A database system which will allow members of the public to access information. Usually a charge is made for the service and subscribers may require special equipment such as modems and terminals.

robot arm   Device which mimics the actions of the human arm with shoulder, elbow and wrist joints. The hand may have a gripper or may be equipped with sensors or other devices. The movements are often controlled by a computer connected to electric motors, hydraulic rams or pneumatic systems.

Telecom Gold   Public electronic mail system operated by British Telecom. Subscribers are given an electronic mailbox into which their messages are received and they can trasmit messages to other subscribers.

Index